In God's Mercy
My Spiritual Journey

D1302057

by *Linda Lint*
with *Marichelle Roque-Lutz*
and the *Rev. James W. Kofski*

A Not Forgotten Publication

About the Cover

The cover of this book is based on images from Linda's dreams and on reflections on her life.

The storm clouds and turbulent sea represent the challenges and difficulties of her life.

The cross represents her faith in Jesus' help in the midst of her trials.

The rays represent the grace earned by Christ's blood and water shed on the cross to provide for God's mercy and our salvation.

Linda's husband, Larry, provided the photographs used in the cover design by Teman Cooke.

The sea photo was taken from the deck of the USS Guam LPH 9 during Operation Desert Storm.

The sky photo was taken in Wexford, Pennsylvania, two days after Larry was spared from injury in a snowstorm driving incident.

The cross is from the top of Our Mother of Perpetual Help Church in Ephrata, Pennsylvania, Linda's current parish.

Front cover art by Teman Cooke
http://thcooke.com + teman@thcooke.com

Internal design and layout by Alice S. Morrow Rowan

Produced by Not Forgotten Publishing Services
NotForgottenPublishing@gmail.com

Available at https://www.createspace.com/4289387
and at Amazon.com

Printed in the United States of America

Contents

Introduction

When I was in my teens, I loved to engage in gossip to entertain myself and to make myself more popular. I was unmindful of whether I destroyed the reputations of people around me. As I grew older, I committed graver sins involving lies and hypocrisy. I have repented and confessed these same sins many, many times. I have prayed a lot for myself as well as for the people I offended, but I know I am still a sinner.

In spite of my sins, I have had visions and dreams about Jesus and the Blessed Mother. When I first had these dreams, I wondered why I had them, because as a sinner I felt unworthy. I usually could interpret the dreams I had while living in Egypt. But the ones that have occurred in the United States have sometimes puzzled me. They have been different.

For example, in 2007 I had a strange dream. People were coming to our house bringing books to be signed by the Rev. James W. Kofski (Father Jim), my spiritual director since my days in Egypt. Afterward, while meditating on a book written by Monsignor Felix A. Losito, wondering about the meaning of my dreams, and praying that God would give me a sign about what to do with them, I had a vision of the Blessed Mother telling me to write my entire story and not hold back anything.

Before the dream, I had written about 10 pages that I intended to be read only by my daughter, Maryann. I wanted her to know how God had interacted in my life, but I took care to mention only the good I did. Maybe the Virgin wanted me to add more pages. But I put it off and then conveniently forgot about it.

The dreams did not stop. In one dream, my husband, my daughter, and I were on a pilgrimage. People were looking at the sky hoping for an apparition. We got tired of waiting and decided to go home. As soon as we left the place, I saw Jesus inside a crystal glass. He appeared as the image of the Divine Mercy, with red and blue rays streaming down from his heart, just as he had showed himself to Saint Faustina. I cried. Covering my mouth, I mentioned Jesus' name a couple of times. When I woke up, my face was wet with tears.

In another dream, Jesus was agreeing with the Blessed Mother that I needed to write my story, including the dreams and visions I'd had, so that people who read it would know the transforming power of God's mercy. Despite these signs and dreams, I did not want to do it. I was afraid that people would judge me and say I was making it all up. If I had a choice, I would rather have 10 times the pain of first-time childbirth than open my life to everyone.

A year later, I was at school teaching as a substitute when I experienced a terrible pain and could not stand up. My aide told me to go home, but I told her I would stay until the end of the class.

The pain continued, so my husband, Larry, brought me to our family doctor. A series of tests, including an ultrasound, showed I had ovarian cancer. I put down my head to pray. If God would heal me, I bargained with Him and the Blessed Mother, I would finish writing my story.

My doctor then ordered an MRI to see if the findings would match those of the ultrasound. The MRI results came back negative. My doctor and his physician assistant, both Catholics, were surprised. They told me they believed a miracle had occurred.

I knew then that God had spared me in order for me to trust Him and finish this book as a testimony to His goodness. In God's mercy, He will forgive us, as long as we are sincerely sorry for our sins and try our best not to sin again. ✞

PART ONE

1
Our Lady of Piat

My grandmother, Felipa Medrano, was a well-to-do woman in Aparri, Cagayan Province, located in the northeasternmost part of the Philippines. She didn't approve of my father, because he came from a poor family. However, my father, Victorio Martin, worked hard and managed to finish a liberal arts degree in order to be worthy of my mother, Tarcila, who had a degree in elementary education. He also managed my grandmother's store and other businesses. He received no salary. My grandmother—my Lelang—thought it was enough payment that she housed and fed us.

I was the oldest child and dearly loved by my Lelang. I also was a sickly baby and often had to be brought to the doctor. Because she paid for these doctor visits, Lelang told my parents that she was going to take me away from them. This was a wake-up call for Papang, my father. Tired of my grandmother maltreating him, he accepted a job offer from her cousin, who was head petitioner of the Bureau of Lands in that part of the Philippines.

Lelang's cousin encouraged Papang to look for untitled vacant lands and petition the government for them. One of my earliest memories was going with my parents on one of these trips. I was 5 years old. We were sailing on the Pacific Ocean close to the foot of the Sierra Madre mountain range when our *banca,* a canoelike boat with outriggers, capsized. Everyone made it to the shore except me. I remember being pulled away from under the capsized boat by a Negrito, an indigenous native of the Sierra Madres. When I surfaced, I saw Mamang—my mother—on the shore, crying. She thought I had drowned. In her hands she tightly held a

3

picture of Our Lady of Piat, which she had seen floating by her as she made her way to shore.

Our Lady of Piat, one of the Blessed Mother's titles in the Philippines, is venerated throughout the country. A lot of miracles have been attributed to her. On July 2, her feast day, the statue of Our Lady of Piat is paraded in the municipality of Piat in Cagayan Province. It is said that when the Lady wants to be in procession, three children can easily carry her statue. And if she doesn't, even 20 adults cannot carry her.

Mamang was very devoted to the Lady of Piat, and I believe the Lady answered her prayers and created a miracle that day. What Mamang didn't know was I had been safely floating under the capsized *banca*, playing and enjoying myself, unaware of the dangers I faced. I had actually been upset when the Negrito pulled me out. ✝

2
Other Early Childhood Memories

I went to an American school in Aparri for kindergarten, and to a public school for grades one and two. As early as age 6 or 7, I started reading *The Book of Judgment.* Lelang had hidden the book from me, but I found it. One day she caught me and told me I was forbidden to read the book because I was still young and would not understand.

In *The Book of Judgment,* I saw pictures of God the Father holding a scale that weighs your sins, with your guardian angel standing behind you and the devil lurking at the left side waiting to see if you belong to him. I understood at that early age that if I belonged to God, my guardian angel would assist me to heaven; and if I belonged to the devil, my guardian angel would cry and the devil would take me into a pit of fire. I also saw a picture of souls of children who had died without being able to repent, and they were blaming and cursing their parents because the parents did not do a good job of disciplining them.

When I was 8, we moved away from my grandmother's home to the adjacent province of Isabela. I finished my primary and elementary education in Maconacon, a town my Papang founded there. I remember walking a kilometer to school every day, rain or shine, when I was in third grade. If I was sick but was able to walk, I still tried to go to school because Mamang instilled in me very early on the importance of education. She told me it is the one inheritance nobody can take away from me.

At that time I already had an idea that I needed to study hard so I could earn money to help my family buy food. Because Papang, as the town founder, was the head petitioner for the people, he kept traveling to process papers for tilling virgin land. This left Mamang alone to take care of us. The search for food was a day-to-day problem and there were times when we were hungry. I remember Mamang dividing the food among her five children and herself. I remember my brother Herbert crying so hard when his tiny piece of meat fell from his plate and our dog ate it. That was his share for the day and Mamang had nothing else to give him.

Now and then Papang's friends gave us *kamote* (sweet potato) and *kamoteng kahoy* (cassava) to eat. But we were used to eating rice. So, whenever a boat arrived from Cagayan, Mamang rushed to check whether Lelang remembered us. She had many hectares of land planted with rice. Each harvest season, her tenants gave her many *cavans* (50 kg sacks) of rice, her share as the landowner. Lelang gave my uncle several *cavans* but nothing for us. She was still punishing Papang for moving us away from her.

Being the eldest, I made decisions for my siblings from a very young age. Also, because of my persistence in my studies, I got very good grades and was valedictorian four times. At that young age, I already had in my mind how I was going to help my family. I was going to earn money for them. That's why I studied hard. ☦

3
High School

After graduating from elementary school, I was sent back to my grandmother in Aparri. There was no high school near Maconacon at that time; and even if there had been, my parents did not have money to educate me further.

Lelang was pleased because she finally got me. My daily routine was to get the merchandise ready for display in her store, to sweep the floors, and to cook for her and my uncle.

Lelang was very, very religious. Living with her, I developed a sense of closeness to God, the Blessed Mother, and the saints. From her I heard for the first time stories from the Old and New Testaments. I knew she wanted me to be a nun because she often told me how desirable convent life is. She said nuns are protected from the evils of society. All they have to do is pray and when they die they will go to heaven.

Lelang abstained from eating meat every Tuesday. During Holy Week, she ate only once a day, and on Good Friday she didn't eat anything. It was from her that I learned how to fast and to abstain, practices I follow to this day. From her I also learned how to chant the *pasion* (Passion story). Every day of Holy Week our neighbors joined us for the *pasion.* It is a Filipino tradition that continues to this day.

✤

My grandma, accompanied by my uncle, traveled from Aparri to Tuao to visit her rice lands and settle problems with tenants. Whenever they went, they left me alone in the big house for two days or more. At night I felt scared and could hardly sleep. So I went to my Lelang's bedroom and took her 24-inch-high statues, including the statues of the Santo Niño (Holy Child), the Blessed Mother, and St. Anthony. I placed them around me on my bed and I wasn't afraid anymore. During one of these nights, some neighbors asked me if we had a guest. They said they had seen a fair woman wearing a white dress in the window of my bedroom, where I lay asleep.

One night, I heard footsteps downstairs. Then a strong wind blew the kerosene light inside my bedroom, even when all my windows were closed. I was scared in spite of the statues lying on my bed. The next morning I approached our guidance counselor, who was also a nun, and told her about my dreams and frightening experiences. She said I needed to memorize the Apostles Creed and recite it each time I felt scared. That helped. I didn't pray the rosary every day at that time, but I always recited the Apostles Creed.

Aside from often dreaming about Jesus, the Blessed Mother, and the saints, nothing distinguished me from other teenagers. I was growing up and discovering myself and my self-worth. I was headstrong, arrogant, and argumentative. One time I answered Lelang back in front of my parents. Instead of scolding me for my disrespect, Lelang scolded Papang for spoiling me.

In reply, Papang got a 2-by-2 piece of wood and beat me hard several times in front of Lelang. I could hardly stand up afterward. I was stunned. Papang had never hit me hard before. Of course he did this just to satisfy my Lelang, but I didn't know that then.

After the beating I went to the cabinet where my uncle kept the pesticide Polydol. I went under the house and drank the contents of the bottle. Luckily what I drank was not enough to kill me immediately. As I lay there, I heard my family yelling out my name. "Where are you?" they shouted. Somehow they felt I was in trouble. I heard Papang tell Mamang that he would not have hit me but he felt he had to satisfy Lelang. I was happy thinking that if I did die, they would be sad. But they found me in time and brought me to the hospital.

My suicide attempt happened when I was in first-year high school at St. Paul's College. I had never made my confession before, but was about to. It was mandatory in a Catholic school. The nuns prepared me on what to say and what to expect.

"Bless me, Father, for I have sinned. This is my first confession," I began. Then I listed all my sins: I was disobedient to my grandmother and my parents, I quarreled with my brothers, I lied, I was a hypocrite, I gossiped.

"And . . . ah . . . I . . . ah . . . drank poison because I wanted to die."

Through the little holes in the window that separated the priest and me, I saw him start up.

"Ohhhh!" he said in a big, low voice. "That is a BIG sin. WHY DID YOU DO IT?"

I was sure everybody in the church heard him. I was so frightened that I ran out of the confessional box and slid into one of the pews beside another classmate. The priest emerged and started looking for me around the church, but he couldn't find me because my veiled head was bowed low as if in prayer.

I did not wait to be absolved and did not receive my penance. So much for my first confession. Two weeks later, when mandatory confession time came again, I enumerated all my sins once more, ending with "I drank poison because I wanted to die."

This time I was aware that I had committed a big sin. Had I died I would have gone directly to hell for trying to kill myself. Thank goodness the priest who heard my confession was nicer. He admonished me in a soft voice before giving me my penance. I don't remember now what it was. I am so grateful to God that He allowed me to live and to repent of my big sin and confess it to a priest.

Afterward, I went regularly to confession and received Holy Communion. I also became devoted to St. Anthony of

Padua because the saint's chapel was just beside Lelang's house. I made daily stops and prayed to him to help me in my studies. As a result, I was one of five students in my class who passed the national college entrance exams. ✝

4
College Life and First Jobs

I went to St. Paul University in Tuguegarao, the capital of Cagayan Province, for a business management degree. However, after just one semester, I decided I needed to help my family financially. I got work as a secretary in the municipal office. After office hours, I also taught shorthand and typing at Acme Vocational School.

In a few months I became a full-time employee at Acme. In addition to teaching, I worked as secretary to Acme's owner, Eric Patterson. Eventually he also entrusted me to help run his cinema and poultry business.

My boss made me count how much money we earned for his businesses as well as the rest of the money in his safe. I think he was testing me. But with all these hundreds of thousands that passed my hands, I did not take a single penny, even though my salary was only 800 pesos a month (or $40; at that time the exchange rate was 20 pesos to $1).

Mr. Patterson was a millionaire in Scotland. He told me he wanted to bring me with him to his country to help him manage his other businesses there. To his disappointment, I decided to quit Acme and go back to St. Paul University. I felt I needed to stand up and work for my own future. My motto at that time was, "Others can; why can't I?"

Around this time young men started courting me. I was so arrogant and uncharitable that if the young man did not fit my standard of "smart" and "successful," I tore up his letter in front of him or embarrassed him in other ways. At that age, I was very far removed from praying and including God in whatever decisions I made. I was miles away from asking blessings before eating, praying before cooking that God would bless the people who ate the food, and wearing sacramental medals like the Miraculous Medal and the crucifix, even while asleep.

However, I still wanted to be a nun. Besides my business subjects, I took Theology 1 to 8. Immediately after graduation, Mila, who was my best friend in college, and I planned to enter the convent. Because we had gone to college, we knew we would not just clean and do household chores. We would work in an office, teach, and possibly travel abroad. I don't speak for Mila, who is now a nun teaching in the same university we graduated from. My idea at that time on entering the convent was to avoid marriage since my grandmother's friend told me I would die in childbirth. ✞

5
Change of Attitude

Going to a Catholic school did not cure me of my faults. I thought I was a nice person because I sang in the church choir and joined the Legion of Mary. I also was a member of the glee club and joined the musical *Showboat* when St. Paul University's theater club presented it. I was quite popular and received my share of attention from the young men. And I loved to see guys "crying" because of me.

Then a series of events happened that changed my inflated sense of my holiness. One day on my way to school, an old woman approached me at the gate begging for money to buy food. I had 20 pesos with me and no loose change, so I brushed her off saying I didn't have money.

That night in the boarding house I could not find my tuition fee. I had to go to the principal's office and write a promissory note in order to take my exams. No one in the boarding house knew what had happened to my tuition money. However, one of my classmates said he would bring me to somebody who would know.

That somebody was Rica, his cousin. He told me Rica had the gift of healing. She would go into a trance and the Blessed Mother would use her to heal. My classmate said Rica had healed many people, including terminal patients from the provincial hospital. People also went to Rica for answers to their problems.

I went to Rica to find out who had taken my tuition money. I joined a roomful of people praying rosary after rosary. Finally Rica's body stiffened. Her eyes closed and her mouth began to move. Someone whispered that the Blessed Mother had taken possession of her. While Rica was in a trance, we took turns asking her questions.

"Who took my tuition money?" I asked her.

Still in a trance, Rica said, "Do you remember an old woman who asked you for money to buy food because she was hungry, but you ignored her?"

I wondered how she knew and I became frightened, but I replied, "Yes."

Rica said, "The reason you lost your tuition money was because you were not generous." She paused and said, "She was the Blessed Mother in disguise to test your heart and your attitude."

Rica said she was going to tell me who took my money but only if I promised to pray for this girl and not ask her to return the money to me because she did it out of necessity. "You need to change your ways," she said.

I cried then and continued crying for many days. How did she know about the incident when I hadn't told her about it? I was positive it was the Blessed Mother talking to me through Rica.

I became Rica's friend after that visit. Sometimes I spent the weekend in her house. I found out how self-sacrificing she was. During Holy Week she started her fast on Holy Monday and didn't eat anything solid until Easter Sunday. I realized how close to the Blessed Mother she was. She often went downstairs to pray before a life-size statue of Mary and ask for advice about what to do with her life.

With Rica's help and influence, I tried to become more humble and charitable. I shared my money to the point that for one whole year I bought my roommate's food and cooked for her.

After graduation in 1983, I ran to Mamang to tell her about my plans to be a Paulinian nun. Excited, I told her that as a nun with an education I would be able to travel to all St. Paul colleges in the Philippines and possibly abroad. Mamang looked at me without smiling and gave out an emphatic no.

"If you are a nun," she said, "you cannot even buy your own shoes. And we expect you to find a job and support your three brothers in college."

When I was working I did not see even a shadow of the money I earned. Everything went to my mother. Now that I had graduated, she expected me to continue helping the family.

In the Philippines one cannot enter the convent without the permission of both parents. So I had to abandon my ambition to become a nun. Although I was not a nice person—I mean I was a hypocrite and thought I was better than most—I was raised to respect and obey my parents. And that was that.

Mamang ordered me to go back home to Isabela and find a job. I applied at Acme Vocational School once again. The business was now owned by Mr. Patterson's son. He hired me as a secretary. Six months later there was a massive layoff and I was out of a job. Mr. Patterson's son said I could stay if I took the job of a friend in the personnel department. I could not do that because I knew her family needed the money more than mine. So I chose to be laid off. ✟

6
Lost in Manila

In 1984, I decided to find employment overseas. I went to my uncle to borrow money to go to Manila for this venture. He loaned me 2,000 pesos (about $100 at the peso-to-dollar exchange rate then). Merly, who was my close friend at that time, accompanied me to Manila. She said I could stay with her older sister, Cynthia (not her real name), together with her mother and her youngest brother, Rolly (not his real name).

Because I'd never been to the capital city of the Philippines, Cynthia told Rolly to accompany me to the different government offices to secure my clearances and other papers needed for my application to go abroad.

I also was excited to find out that Cynthia worked at Camp Aguinaldo, the headquarters of the Philippine Army. She interviewed women for positions at the Women's Auxiliary Corps of the Philippines. If my plans to go abroad did not pan out, I told her, I was interested in being a WAC so long as I would be assigned an office job. She said that with my degree, this was possible.

Almost as soon as I moved in with Merly's family, Rolly started courting me. I laughed because it was too ridiculous. He was only in second-year high school and seemed to have no plans to finish studying. I had a business administration degree. He was nothing compared to the other men courting me then.

One of these men was Noli. After I graduated from college and moved back to my parents' home in Maconacon, I promised Noli I'd give him a hopeful answer the next time we met. Then I found out that Cynthia and Noli's sister were very good friends. I also found out that Noli had left Aparri and was living in Manila.

Cynthia called Noli and set a date for us to meet. Noli told me he had a good job as an engineer and was ready to marry me. I said I would think about it. When Rolly heard that I had met a suitor, he became angry and confronted me. I thought I had made it clear to him that I was not interested in him. Then one day, when we were alone in the house, Rolly caught me off guard and assaulted me. I fought until my arms were bruised from struggling. My pleas for him to stop fell on deaf ears. He said he was in love with me and knew this was the only way I would agree to marry him.

I ran to my room, too upset to reply. I felt violated and dirty. But if he thought I was going to marry him, he was dreaming. I had to get as far away from Rolly as I could. As I made plans to leave Cynthia's house, I remembered what Mamang told me: "If a man touches you, you have to marry him." The same thing had happened to my parents. When Papang kissed Mamang and Lelang found out about it, she ordered them to get married. Lelang commanded this even when she disliked Papang.

So, I remained at Cynthia's house. I canceled my next meeting with Noli without explaining why I didn't want to see him again. And my involvement with Rolly became deeper and deeper. I didn't know how to get out of the situation, because he had already told his relatives about us. The issue was public. A few years later, after I went back to Maconacon, my sister-in-law told me that Rolly's mother had been in connivance with him. They had planned what happened to me.

✝

As I write this, I want to find a good reason for why I decided to stay. I guess it was a sense that I had to do what was proper. As Mamang had said, I had to marry him. We went to Tuguegarao and approached Attorney Soriano, a well-known lawyer who was also a family friend, to marry us in a civil ceremony. Instead of consenting to marry us, he rebuked Rolly. He told Rolly he should be ashamed to think he could marry someone with a college degree when he hadn't even finished high school. "What will you feed her?" the lawyer said.

Because Attorney Soriano saw my disappointment, he made an affidavit of intent to marry "when the right time comes." Rolly and I signed this paper in the presence of two witnesses. Then Attorney Soriano turned to me and said, "Linda, one day you will thank me for not consenting to this union."

In 2000, when I went home to the Philippines to introduce my husband and my daughter to my family, we were met at the airport in Tuguegarao by Attorney Soriano. He looked approvingly at Larry and at Maryann and whispered to me, "You see, I made the right decision for you."

The relationship was difficult from the very beginning. Rolly went back to school and wasn't working, so we had to rely on his mother and Cynthia for all our needs. His mother also maltreated and verbally abused me. To remedy the situation, I applied for a job at Philippine Air Force College of Aeronautics, where Rolly went to school. I got the position of secretary at the registrar's office. At night I taught stenography, typing, and personality development.

It was at about this time that I discovered Rolly was a womanizer. This wasn't Rolly's only fault, of course. He was a spoiled mama's boy and he had a violent temper. But I believed, just like other Filipinas of my generation, that the success of a family relies on the woman. I helped him with his studies, hoping he would finish high school and possibly go to college.

Eventually I became pregnant and things started getting worse. After giving birth to our daughter, Jerilyn, I decided to leave him and go back to Cagayan. I left my baby in my uncle and aunt's care so I could work at Northwestern College in the adjacent province of Ilocos Norte. Barely a week later I received an urgent telegram from my aunt. Rolly had arrived and he was threatening to take Jerilyn. I rushed back to find out that Rolly had kicked my uncle so hard he'd broken my uncle's back. Rolly wanted me to go back with him to Manila. Much as I hated to, I said yes because he warned me that if I refused, he would throw a grenade at my uncle's house.

I knew Rolly meant what he'd said. Fearing for my uncle's safety, I went back with Rolly to Cynthia's house. Life there became worse, but I had to bear it because I became pregnant again. I decided that after I gave birth to my second child, I would go home to my parents in Maconacon, leave my children with them, and apply to go abroad for a second time. And that's what I did.

A month after I left him, Rolly wrote me a conciliatory letter. He said he would go to Maconacon and we could start a new life there, instead of staying with his family. That seemed a better solution to my problems than leaving my children and going abroad. So I went back to Manila to fetch Rolly against the advice of my mother and brothers, who disliked him for what he did to my uncle.

Rolly did try his best. He got a stable job and we were able to build our own house. However, he was in continuous conflict with Mamang and my brothers, particularly Danny. It got to the point where Rolly and Danny decided to fight it out in a duel. I knew my brother as well as I knew Rolly and I feared it would end with one of them dead. So I convinced Rolly to go back to Manila. I told him I would visit him as often as I could.

After Rolly left, I worked as a representative of the Department of Social Work in Maconacon. Part of my job was to take care of the town's problems and calamities whenever the municipal mayor was on assignment else-where. I also had to fly each month to the provincial office to submit my monthly report. I took advantage of the free plane tickets to visit Rolly in Manila. The first time I visited him, his sister-in-law told me he was fooling around with other women. I confronted him and told him I wanted out of the relationship. In reply, he pointed a gun at me. "I would rather kill you than see you with another man," he threatened. The second time he pointed the gun at me, his other sister, Tess, was present and was able to grab the gun away.

I went back to Maconacon carrying these heavy burdens. I could not concentrate at work, so I reduced my workload. I also had problems with Mamang. She was very strict with the kids, especially when I was at work.

The last time I visited Rolly, his mother was especially mean to my children. She played favorites and several times gave food to her other grandchildren but not to my kids. Rolly was also trying to get back at me for Mamang's maltreatment of him when he was in Maconacon.

However, something true and liberating happened on this trip. Rolly finally admitted that there was another woman in his life after I found a picture of the woman in his wallet. When I showed it to him, he taunted me that this woman was better educated than me. One would think that Rolly would now allow me to go, but that was not the case. Because I'd borne his children, he felt he owned me. I had to find a way to leave without his knowledge.

One day Rolly went to Clark Air Base in the province of Pampanga and would not return until late afternoon. This was my chance. I asked permission from his mother to visit my cousin, who lived in Fort Bonifacio at the other end of Manila. Jerilyn, barely 2 years, held on to my skirt while I carried Jerry, who was about 8 months, as well as our luggage. I hailed a *jeepney* and struggled to lift Jerilyn into it while holding on to my luggage and carrying Jerry. Thankfully, an old lady materialized from behind me, saw my plight, and helped me.

At the gate of Fort Bonifacio, I left my luggage with the guard because I had to walk a long way to my cousin's house inside the base. I asked my cousin to lend me money so the kids and I could go back to Maconacon immediately. She did so without hesitation. In Maconacon, another cousin who knew about my problems with Rolly approached me and said she would lend me money if I wanted to go abroad.

I immediately said yes, remembering the time I consulted a holy woman about my problems with Rolly. She said the Blessed Mother told her to give me a medal. I was to use it for my protection because, the holy woman said, "You are going so far away." At that time I had abandoned all plans to go abroad, but apparently the Blessed Mother told her to say that to me.

☦

I resigned from my job and once again returned to Manila, but this time it was not to visit Rolly. Before doing so, my father and I stopped by my uncle's house and left Jerilyn and Jerry in their care. From my uncle's house I took the bus to Manila. As I boarded the bus, I could not look back at 2-year-old Jerilyn, who was screaming "Mommy, Mommy," and Jerry, who was 9 months old. My eyes were blinded with tears. I quietly sobbed at the thought I would not see them for a very long time. To console myself, I kept on repeating, "I'm doing this for you, my babies."

I applied as a tutor in Kuwait. While waiting for my visa in Manila, I stayed in the house of the travel agency owner. Some in my group got their visa after two weeks. I got mine after three months. There was a reason for the delay, according to Sister Thelma, a lady with healing powers who visited the travel agency.

She told me, "You need to go to the man you are currently involved with and say sorry for cutting off your relationship." I refused to do it, but the agency owner begged me to heed Sister Thelma. I think she wanted me out of her house. So I sent Rolly a letter. I promised that when I came back from abroad I would marry him, but only if he changed his ways. Three days after I mailed the letter, I got my visa.

Before flying out of the Philippines in 1989, I went to the Church of the Holy Nazarene in downtown Manila to confess all my sins, particularly the sins I committed in Manila. Tears of repentance flowed copiously down my face as I confessed. I then promised myself that I would not get married or have anything to do with men.

In Manila I lost my innocence and my pride of self. Most important, I lost the special connection I had with God, Jesus, the Blessed Mother, and all the saints before Rolly took over my life. Even when I prayed the rosary and made novenas to St. Rita and Our Mother of Perpetual Help in Baclaran, Manila, it seemed they did not answer my prayers.

I did not realize then that God didn't grant the specific favors I prayed for because he had different plans for me. Better plans. ✞

Our Lady of Piat

Aparri elementary school administration
building with classrooms behind

Aerial view of Maconacon, approaching from Divilacan Bay,
with Sierra Madre mountains in background

Maconacon elementary school

St. Paul University Tuguegarao, main building

St. Paul University garden

Linda at St. Paul graduation ceremony,
March 20, 1983

Attorney Soriano at home

PART TWO

7

Kuwait

I left the Philippines for Kuwait on December 8, 1989, the feast of the Immaculate Conception. I was very excited at the prospect of starting a new life in another country. Immediately after landing in Kuwait, I called my employer and heard children's voices in the background. In my mind, these were the children I was hired to tutor.

However, as soon as I reached my employer's home, the very first thing my employer asked me to do was to iron his big Arab robe. I told him I didn't know how to iron. I learned to cook and clean for my grandmother, but we had a laundry woman do the washing and ironing. My employers then told me they hadn't hired me to tutor their children.

They told me to pair their children's socks. It seemed easy but all the socks looked alike and I wasn't much good at finding which piece matched the other. Next they ordered me to wash their delicate clothes by hand. I did, up to the point that my hands bled. I confess I wasn't much good at doing this. I did not want to do this. I wanted to teach and tutor.

I arrived during Ramadan and that meant more work for me. My employers didn't eat from sunrise to sunset, but after 6 p.m. they continuously ate until 4 a.m. and I had to tend to their needs. They installed a bell in my room so they could easily contact me whenever they needed me to serve them food. I probably slept only a full hour each night, and I was dead tired. I figured out how to get more sleep by going to the bathroom and turning on the faucet for at least 20 minutes, pretending I was taking a shower when I was actually sleeping.

I imagined hell would be something like I was experiencing, but magnified a thousand times. And I gathered God allowed me to experience just a bit of what hell would be like if I died without His forgiving mercy.

I was in this horrible situation for almost two months before I had the courage to tell my employers to bring me back to my agency. In reply, they called a policeman. The policeman asked me in a stern voice why I didn't want to work anymore. I told him why. Angrily he told me to get in his car. I had heard from others that if a Kuwaiti policeman brought a woman to prison, he could rape her first. My heart started to beat very fast but I decided to place myself in God's protection. I told myself He was in control, not the policeman.

In the car I prayed to the Santo Niño. The Holy Child is loved and worshiped in the Philippines because of the many miracles attributed to him. When I was a teenager, I saw the real Holy Child, not the statue, in my parents' home in Maconacon. I was in the living room and awake when I saw this child. His face was like a round, red apple and he had very beautiful eyes. I pinched myself to make sure I wasn't dreaming.

The next day, I joined my sister-in-law Lydia as well as the neighbors in their regular Sunday afternoon prayer in front of the Santo Niño. Lydia fell into a trance. Then she spoke in a child's voice. The neighbors said the Santo Niño took possession of Lydia. I asked the Santo Niño if I really did see him the day before. Speaking in a child's voice, Lydia said, "Yes."

In the policeman's car, I prayed to the Santo Niño to protect me. I also prayed to St. Benedict with a special prayer in Latin that the holy woman I consulted in Manila gave me for my protection. I was too concentrated on my prayers that I didn't notice where the policeman brought me. To my surprise he stopped in front of my agency. I thanked him and walked in as fast as I could.

The agency manager took pity on me when I explained that my employers forced me to do a lot of manual work, which wasn't part of my job description. He said I could stay with him and his wife until he got me a better employer. While I was at the agency, two Filipinas came in with broken ribs. They had been forced to clean the higher windows of their employer's house, lost their balance while they were cleaning, and fell to the ground. That night we all slept at the agency. I heard them crying from their pain. I thanked the Santo Niño and St. Benedict for not allowing something like that to happen to me.

The following day the owner of the agency brought me to his home. The Filipina who worked for him was surprised to see me. She said that was the first time her employer had brought anybody home. She teased me saying her employer must have seen an angel on my face. And so I knew that God was taking care of me.

Two weeks later the manager of the agency found me a job working for a childless husband and wife who traveled a lot. The wife particularly was often away because she was an accountant for Kuwait Airways. Rather than have to go back to the Philippines after only two months in Kuwait, I accepted the offer.

I worked for Raj and Nadine Ali (not their real names) about five months before I knew I had to leave them as well. The dilemma this time was not overwork and lack of consideration for my welfare. It was just the opposite. Nadine traveled a lot so Raj and I were alone in their house. Raj tried to seduce me a number of times. Each time, I was able to repel him by telling him he was a married man and what he was doing was wrong.

Then Raj told me he would divorce Nadine if I told him I liked him and would marry him. Raj's brother-in-law was happily married to a Filipina. This probably was the reason he kept on pressing me to give in to him. One day, in frustration, Raj told me he could force me and I wouldn't be able to do anything about it because nobody was there to defend me. I told myself yes, there was. God was always with me to protect me.

In July 1990, my employers went to France. On July 2, the feast of Our Lady of Piat, I went to Egypt to live with Nadine's sister. Their plan was to get me back once they returned to Kuwait. It never happened. On August 2, the Iraqis invaded Kuwait. So, when Raj and Nadine Ali returned from France, they went straight to Egypt.

I heard what had happened in Kuwait from a Filipina. She and her Egyptian husband were in Kuwait at the time of the invasion but were able to escape back to Egypt. She said some of the Filipinas who sought shelter in the Philippine Embassy in Kuwait had been raped by Iraqis. The soldiers were raping Kuwaiti women as well and killing babies incubated in the hospital. I left Kuwait at the right time. Again, God had intervened on my behalf.

I stayed with my employers in Egypt for another two months. During that time Raj asked me to marry him almost daily. It got so unbearable that I decided to call the Philippine Embassy in secret and ask for help. I was fortunate that Consul Orestes Bello himself picked up the phone. When he heard about my problem, he told me to get away as fast as I could and go to the embassy. That night I prayed to God to help me escape very soon because I was afraid my employer would use force on me and I wouldn't be able to defend myself.

The next day an amazing thing happened. Raj ordered me to bring his food to his office on the first floor. This was unusual because he always went upstairs for lunch. As I fixed his meal, I realized this was God's answer to my prayer. I had been ordered to stay inside on the second floor of the apartment and certainly never to go down to the first floor. Until that day.

Quickly I called Consul Bello to tell him I was going to make my escape that day. He said he and his wife were going to wait for me at the embassy. I pocketed all the money I had, about $60. I didn't change out of my house clothes, to avoid suspicion. Then I went down to the office and gave my employer his lunch. Slowly and naturally, I left the office, snuck out the back door, and hailed a taxi. I told the driver I would pay him $50 to bring me as fast as he could to the Philippine Embassy.

I was so scared that Raj Ali would discover I was gone and drive out after me before I reached the safety of the consulate. If he caught me, he could have me imprisoned. I arrived a little past 5 p.m. at the Philippine Embassy, and there were Consul and Mrs. Bello waiting for me. ✝

8
At the Philippine Embassy in Egypt

Consul Bello directed me to go to the second floor, where the other refugees stayed, and advised me not to go to the ground floor for any reason. He was afraid my employer would go to the consulate, find me, and grab me. And indeed, Raj did come to the consulate looking for me. For that reason I wasn't able to attend Mass for a couple of weeks.

At that time there was a memo from the Philippine government ordering Filipinos affected by the Kuwait war to go home whether they liked it or not. I didn't want to go home because I had not earned enough to pay back the money I borrowed from my cousin to make my trip to Kuwait.

I approached Mrs. Bello, who was the administrative officer of the embassy at that time, and explained my situation. When Mrs. Bello found out I graduated from St. Paul University, a private school run by nuns and priests, she promised to hire me as an assistant secretary and issue me a new passport and a visa.

I started helping the regular secretary by taking notes for the consul in shorthand, preparing invitations for the diplomats' functions, filing papers, taking phone calls, and doing any other secretarial job the embassy wanted me to do.

I also volunteered to lead the staff's mandatory praying of the rosary each evening. Even the three Muslim staffers participated by silently staying with us as we prayed. However, I did not realize there was one Filipina who refused to join in because I was the one leading the rosary.

I found out later that this lady believed she should have been hired instead of me because she had a degree in computer programming. She was so angry and jealous that one night, after dinner, she attempted to stab me with a knife. I was practicing hymns for Mass with two other Filipinas when one of them screamed out my name. She was staring in shock at something behind me. I looked back to see this computer programmer coming at me with a 10-inch knife.

Luckily I knew a bit of basic martial arts. Instinctively I caught the hand that was holding the knife and twisted her wrist while pressing my fingers into the weakest part, to the point that she dropped the knife and couldn't move her hand. After her failed attempt, she went to her partitioned area on the upper floor of the embassy. I could have turned the knife on her but I was thinking at that time that if I did, I could be jailed and be the loser. I think all along I was being protected by God because I again remembered the holy woman who gave me the St. Benedict medal and the protective prayer in Latin.

The following morning, after Consul Bello found out what had happened, he sent the woman away. Everything went back to normal and we prayed the rosary every night.

One evening, as we sat talking before going to bed, one Filipina started trembling and gasping for breath. Her eyes bulged and her mouth frothed. We screamed and cried in fear that she was going to die. Then I felt pushed to pray over her. I again remembered the holy woman in Manila who gave me the St. Benedict medal and the protective prayer. I prayed it for the first time over the stricken Filipina. Instantly she recovered and thanked me for what I did. I thought how like magic the prayer was because I still didn't believe what it could do.

I wrote to my mother about how God had used me to heal the Filipina. She wrote back that my brother Danny was healed this way. The doctors said he had only three months to live. So Mamang brought him to a boy who was known to heal people with prayers. This boy was able to cure Danny instantly. She told me she believed I was used by the Holy Spirit to heal the Filipina. Apparently the boy who healed Danny told Mamang that I was chosen to have healing powers but I refused to use them—until now. ☩

9
God Helps a Filipino-American Family

After helping out a while at the Philippine Embassy, I worked as a nanny for a United Nations representative for almost two years. During this time, I was able to join a pilgrimage to Mount Sinai with the Philippine Embassy staff.

It was a satisfying and memorable experience for me. I stood by the Burning Bush, where God gave the commandments to Moses. I visited St. Catherine Monastery. I also saw the spring of Moses as well as the spring of St. Joseph. It is said that when the Holy Family fled to Egypt to protect the Baby Jesus from King Herod's slaughter of the innocents, Joseph struck the ground with his staff and out bubbled a spring of water to quench their thirst.

I visited St. Anthony Abbot Monastery, located on a steep mountain higher than Mount Sinai. Only one person at a time can get into the cave where St. Anthony fasted and prayed many hours every day. It is said that somebody appeared to him offering him food while he was fasting but he was able to overcome.

I also visited Alexandria, Egypt, where the incorrupt body of St. Bishoy is kept. The monk I spoke to at that place told me St. Bishoy spent more than five hours in prayer every day. I asked the monk why St. Bishoy needed to pray so many hours. He told me that if a person prays most of his waking hours, he won't fall into sin because the Holy Spirit is always with him.

In addition to what I'd heard from the monk, I also heard from Father Abel, our pastor at Holy Family Church at Maadi, Cairo. Father Abel had been a monk at St. Catherine Monastery for 15 years. He told me that the next time I climbed Mount Sinai and visited St. Catherine's, I should ask the monks to intercede with God on my behalf because they are holy and God will listen to them.

I did just that. The second time I climbed Mount Sinai, I asked the priest in charge of St. Catherine Church if I could visit the monks in their cells. The priest hesitated until I told him Father Abel sent me. Inside their quarters, I approached a monk who looked American and so would be able to speak English. I learned that monks are highly educated and are in the monastery for further studies. The Rev. James Kofski (Father Jim), a Maryknoll priest who became my spiritual director, said one of the qualifications of becoming a cardinal is time spent living as a monk.

I told the monk about a Filipino-American family I had met in Egypt. Let us call them John and Connie Brown. John had an accident at the American company where he was a contractual engineer, and his legs were amputated as a result. The company denied him medical care because he was still under probation when the accident happened. The company also held his family's passports.

I asked the monk if he could pray for the Browns because they were desperate. The Filipino-American couple who had been helping them had returned to the United States for good, and they had asked me to provide what help I could to the Browns. I brought the family milk almost every day. The first time I presented the milk to them, Connie's babies, ages 1 1/2 years and 6 months, grabbed the milk from me because they were very hungry. I could not hold back my tears, remembering my own two babies I had left back home.

I prayed to God to show me a way to help the family. And God did. I asked John to teach my friends and me basic computer skills. The money we paid him was enough to pay a month's rent, but they still owed six months of back rent.

Then I was able to convince an officer of FILCOM, the Filipino community in Cairo, to give them regular help. The community pitched in to buy them a big sack of rice and to pay the balance they owed for their apartment. I took Connie aside and urged her to trust God because God loves them very much. I told her that what was happening to them was just a trial.

I also said she and John needed to change their ways and learn to be more humble, go to confession, and go to Mass every Sunday—and God would do the rest. Each Sunday I fetched her and her babies to attend Mass at the Philippine Embassy. At that time I was in charge of making sure there was a priest to say Mass every Sunday for the embassy staff.

A few months later, Connie arrived at the embassy bringing food and clothing for Filipino refugees housed there. She said she was giving back for all the help FILCOM had given her. She told me she had promised God she would be generous and follow God's way. She said an American company in Ismalia, Egypt, had hired John as a computer analyst and supervisor. The company also had him fitted for prosthetic legs.

Much later we learned that the Browns went to the Philippines. Apparently the company John worked for had a sister company in Batangas, Connie's home province. He was hired to run the company. They also were provided with housing. I was so happy for them because again God had proved faithful. He answered the monk's prayers by providing this family with a new job and a new life. But best of all, this family had returned to the faith and had remarried in the Catholic Church. ☦

10
Maadi, Cairo, Egypt

I worked at several jobs to make ends meet. I tutored a third-grader at Cairo American School in Maadi, where the majority of American expatriates live. I also was employed by the consul of the German Embassy as a personal cook, and prepared dishes during diplomat parties.

I lived in the house of Consul Corazon Bahjin, who had taken Consul Bello's place after his term ended. She invited me and a few other Filipinas to stay with her. We were called Bahjin's Angels because we accompanied her wherever she went on weekends.

The last year of Consul Bahjin's term, I was elected secretary of FILCOM. My second pilgrimage to Mount Sinai occurred soon after. It was necessary for me to go because the trip was sponsored by FILCOM and I was a Filipino minister of Holy Family Church in Maadi.

I was grateful to Ling Hicks, president of the Filipino community at that time, because when she and her husband returned for good to the United States, she authorized me to take charge of getting a priest to say Mass at the Philippine Embassy every Sunday at noon. She introduced me to Father Jim, who was then chaplain at the embassy. I assisted him with whatever he needed for the Mass. That's how Father Jim became my buddy and personal spiritual director.

✠

As I had promised myself when I left Manila, I didn't mingle with any men except priests. My bad experience with Rolly in Manila had made me afraid of all men. Besides Father Jim, there were Father Lance, a Maryknoll priest; Father

Abel, a Franciscan priest; Father Mattie, of the Society of African Missions; and Fathers Alberto and Jose, Comboni priests. Father Jose, just like Father Jim, continues to be my friend to this day. If I have concerns and need his wisdom and advice, I write to him or call him long distance in France, where he now serves.

When Father Jim was transferred to Jerusalem in 1994, we did not have a regular priest to say Mass on Sundays. I mentioned this problem to Father Peter, who belonged to the same order as Father Jim. Could he help us? He said I needed permission from the bishop in Alexandria and he gave me the telephone number. I asked the vice president of the Filipino community to call the bishop. Fortunately the bishop promised to send a priest to say Mass every Sunday. It went well for a couple of weeks. Then Ambassador Galenzoga prevented us from using the social hall because, he said, it was going to be renovated. This was bad news for the Filipinos whose visas had expired and were afraid to attend Mass elsewhere. The embassy was the only safe place for them to stay during their weekends off.

Whenever there was no priest to say Mass, a group of Filipino Christians who called their sect Born Again held their own service during the time designated for Mass. Most of the Catholics complained because their teaching was different. They did not venerate the Blessed Mother and they wanted us to throw out our statues and rosaries. So every time no priest was available, I guarded the social hall and did not allow the group to preach during the time designated for Mass.

The leader of the group complained to a top official that I was preventing them from using the consulate hall. They said they were also Filipinos and had the same rights as we did. I did not prevent them from preaching at any other time and I could not understand why they picked the time scheduled for Mass. It was apparent their intentions were to preach negatively about Catholicism and hopefully make a few conversions.

But the day came when the Born Again group did get permission from the ambassador to preach in the social hall whenever there was no priest to say Mass. One Sunday when I wasn't able to contact a priest, I prayed in front of my statue of our Lady of Fatima. I got this statue the first time I went to Jerusalem with my friend Daylin to visit Father Jim. I prayed the rosary and asked the Lady of Fatima to help. I noticed that the face of my statue turned pink and started to glow. I knew then she had heard my prayers and I would be able to stop the Born Again people from preaching at noon.

I went straight to the social hall and told them, "No! You are not allowed to preach!" The administrative officer was behind me when I said this, but he said nothing. This was the day they began to dislike me. But I didn't care, because I was fighting for my Catholic beliefs.

I told Mrs. Medrano, who had been appointed consul after Mrs. Bahjin's term ended, about the problem Catholics at the embassy were facing at that time. Since she was a devout Catholic, she became angry. She said it wasn't really true that there was a renovation going on in the social hall. Consul Medrano personally went to Zamalek, Cairo, and got the Comboni priest, Father Jose, to say Mass for the embassy staff. She also gave me back the responsibility of bringing priests to the embassy every Sunday. The Comboni priests came from the United States, Italy, Mexico, and Sudan. They were in Egypt to study Arabic and French. From then on, I was able to get a different priest every Sunday.

Besides assisting at Mass at the Philippine Embassy, I also attended Mass at Holy Family Church in Maadi, where Father Abel was the parish priest. Sometimes Father Abel also said Mass at the Philippine Embassy. He asked the head of the parish council to approach me about starting a Filipino Mass at Holy Family every Friday at 9 a.m. I ignored the request because I was already assisting at Mass at the Philippine Embassy. I was approached three times. Then one of my older Filipina friends said that if I started it, they would help me. That is how I came to assist at two Masses—one on Sundays at noon and another on Fridays at 9 a.m. Sometimes I got help from the couple who played the organ. But when they went back home to the Philippines, I ended up doing everything.

Whenever I sang at the Friday Mass, I had to receive Communion after the recessional song. One time this didn't happen because Father Abel left before I could catch him. I called Father Alberto. He invited me to attend a special Lenten Mass that day at Saint Joseph Church in Zamalek. The Mass was said specially for 17 priests; therefore, only 17 hosts were prepared to be consecrated. During Communion, Father Alberto divided his Host to share with me. I felt blessed by God with the privilege of attending this solemn Mass with 17 priests.

After Mrs. Bahjin left, I needed to move. Because I was working in Maadi, I decided to look for a place there. After Sunday Mass at the embassy, I asked around and Baket Belen advised me to take an apartment with her daughter Mila and her cousin.

Mila had a son less than a year old. The boy was sick with convulsions, loss of breath, and getting stiff. They had been taking him to Egyptian doctors, but they couldn't figure out the cause. When the boy was sick, Mila and her cousin would scream that the baby was dying. I witnessed this a couple of times but ignored it, because I thought they would take him to the doctor as usual.

One night, I dreamed that I was fighting with the devil. I became stiff and couldn't move until I had the idea to form a cross with my fingers and call out the name of Jesus. Immediately I could move. Then I woke up and got ready for work. I opened the door and found Baket Belen, Mila, her cousin, and the boy standing in front of it. They were screaming and the boy was convulsing. When I looked at his face, he glared at me. His eyes were sharp, they had turned green, and he growled. I knew something was different and I connected the situation with my dream. I felt driven to pray over the boy. As I prayed, he growled louder. When the prayer was finished, he calmed down and I told them not to bring the boy back to the apartment. "You must transfer to another place." I don't know where the words came from, but they did what I said.

So they went to the Philippines and took the child to a person with healing power. He said, "The boy is okay now and it's a good thing she prayed over him or he would be dead. She has a healing power but doesn't like to use it unless there is a situation of life and death." When Baket Belen returned to Egypt, she told me, "I know you have a healing power." I tried to deny it but couldn't because of what the Philippine healer said. I remembered what Tang Totoy said: "Young and old need sacramental medals, especially a crucifix, for protection from evil." After this incident I moved to another apartment in Maadi. ✟

11

First Trip to Israel

I met my husband, Larry, one Wednesday night early in 1994 while attending the Marian novena in honor of Our Lady of Medjugorje at Holy Family Church. One time, while he was walking a group of us Filipinas home, Larry mentioned that he was going to Israel. I was due for a vacation and had intended to go to Israel before going back home to the Philippines. Larry didn't act like the other men around. I was not afraid of him. So I asked Larry quite boldly if I could go with him. With his diplomat status, he—as well as anybody accompanying him—would not have any problem crossing the border from Egypt to Israel. He declined.

Not long after being refused by Larry, I went with parishioners of Holy Family on a second pilgrimage to St. Anthony Abbot Monastery. I climbed the steep mountain to his small cave and there prayed that I could go to Israel soon. Three days later, Daylin called to tell me she was going to pass by Israel on her way home to London for good. Could I join her and could I call Father Jim, who was then chaplain at Mount Zion Convent?

Father Jim gave us his name and address to give to the immigration officer. He also vouched that we were going to Israel only for a pilgrimage. Luckily we passed our interview and were given a one-month visa. We stayed a mere four days; but with Father Jim as our tour guide, we were able to see all the important holy places in Jerusalem and in Bethlehem.

The first time we went to the Holy Sepulcher, I noticed that the glass case of Our Lady of Sorrows contained lots of gold jewelry as well as a diamond ring. Father Jim said the precious items came from people who left them there after their prayers were answered. He told me that if the Lady granted my request, I also had to return and leave something valuable.

It had been five years since I left the Philippines. Although I hadn't forgotten the trauma of living with Rolly, I was ready for another relationship, that is, if marriage was God's plan for my life.

My request, my earnest prayer, was that God would give me a good man, one who could be trusted as one trusted a priest. This was my same prayer at all the holy sites we visited, including the place where Jesus and the apostles celebrated the Passover; the Garden of Olives, where Jesus prayed the night before he was crucified; and the manger in Bethlehem, where Jesus was born. ✝

12
Meeting Larry

As I said in the previous chapter, I met Larry at Holy Family Church. A Filipina who was married to an American had advised Larry that if he wanted to marry a Filipina, he should go to the 9 a.m. Friday Mass and look for the one leading the choir—me. That's how he started to come to that Mass instead of to the Saturday afternoon Mass designated for Americans and the French.

We were introduced when he came to Marian devotion, but I showed no signs of interest in him at that time. Before I met Larry, I turned down the proposal of a Filipino diplomat, Paulo (not his real name). I told him as well as other suitors, including a Filipino-American engineer, an American pilot, and an Egyptian United Nations official, that I wasn't interested in getting married.

I also ignored Larry because I thought he was gay. During Marian devotion, he kept on praying for Steve, his flatmate. Later I learned he was praying for him because Steve's marriage to a Korean woman was in trouble. When Larry's sexual orientation was cleared up, I still ignored him because I thought he was interested in another Filipina. Josie (not her real name) was in charge of the coffee corner and Larry always helped her carry the pot. After devotions, they left together. Larry told me later that they left so he could buy Josie a meal of chicken *tikka*. He said he felt sorry for her because she was always hungry and being maltreated by her employer. He said that was the extent of his interest in her.

In September I arranged for our group to go caroling to raise money to pay for cleaning the church. Larry had just returned from Israel, so we decided to carol at his board-ing house too. Besides his donation, he gave each of us a rosary. Immediately my group noticed the rosary he gave me. It was obviously more expensive than the ones he gave the rest. "He likes you," they teased me.

Our relationship became friendlier when a lady I met in Jerusalem came to Egypt to visit me. Because I had no car to drive her around, I approached Larry to act as tourist guide. Larry said yes, but only if I accompanied them. He reminded me that the lady was my guest, not his.

While my visitor got acquainted with Cairo and its sub-urbs, I got to know Larry close up and realized he was a good man. Mrs. Bahjin warned us that American men were not to be trusted. But Larry was different. I felt safe with him. We became friends and I started inviting him to all Filipino functions. But I also invited the priests who said Mass at the embassy. Sometimes there were two or three Maryknoll or Comboni priests present. The presi-dent of FILCOM assigned me to sit with them and see to their needs. Larry attended these parties but found out he could not dance with me. I was too busy caring for the priests.

One day Larry asked me if I could accompany him to the Philippine Embassy to attend Mass and go to confession. I hesitated because I didn't want to give the embassy staffers something to talk about. These people knew I had two chil-dren in the Philippines and that I had left their father. They did not know Rolly and I were not married. So I had to safe-guard my reputation. They had never seen me alone with any man who wasn't a priest. I didn't want them to conclude that I was fooling around with an American. But Larry want-ed to go to confession, so I said yes. Seeing my initial hesi-tation, Larry said he would go alone and meet me at the embassy before Mass.

True enough, when he came and asked for me, the ad-ministrative officer teased me in Tagalog: "Siguro kasinta-han mo?" (Maybe he's your boyfriend?)

"No! He's a priest," I lied. I gave the same lie to every staffer who asked me the same question. I lied because I believed I would fall from my pedestal as their Filipino minister if they thought I was involved with any man, especially an American.

Larry's contract in Egypt was to end in three weeks. Josie wanted to buy him a going-away present and asked him to go to Khan al Kalili market with her. Larry asked me to accompany them, saying he didn't like to go alone. So I did, but I brought along my gay friend, Mike. The following day Josie told me Larry was her boyfriend. In fact, she told the entire Filipino community.

Meanwhile I decided to give Larry a farewell party in gratitude for touring with my guest as well as for his contributions to the Filipino community. I invited Larry's flatmate, Steve, as well as Josie and most of the Filipinos who helped out in the church. Toward the end of the party, I gave Larry my own farewell gift. It was a papyrus on which I had painstakingly written a poem. I closed with, "Your friend, Linda." He read it and looked quite disappointed.

The following day, Larry invited me to attend the Saturday Anticipatory Mass at Holy Family Catholic Church. After Mass we visited one of my friends, who also gave him a farewell party. Then he asked if I could go to his boarding house with him because he wanted to talk to me about "a serious matter." I said yes.

In his boarding house he asked me why I had closed my dedication on the papyrus with "Your friend, Linda." I said, "Because we're friends." He said he couldn't accept mere friendship. He wanted a closer relationship. Then he formally proposed.

I was surprised. I said Josie told me and everyone else in the Filipino community that she was his girlfriend. Now it was Larry's turn to be surprised. He said he was just being kind and generous whenever he did her a favor. Anyhow, I found myself saying yes to his proposal. The next second

I wanted to take it back. I could not believe that I had accepted. I liked Larry well enough, but getting married to him was another matter. However, I decided not to take back my answer because I was sure nothing would come of it. He was going to America in 10 days and I was leaving Egypt soon to work in Canada.

✝

The next day, I was relieved when Larry told me he would go to Luxor city. However, when he returned a week later, he wanted us to go to Father Abel immediately to tell him about our engagement. That's when it hit me: Larry was serious. A bit panicked, I told Larry I could not make it that day and that if he wanted to, he could go to Father Abel alone. No, he said, he was going to the States in two days and he wanted us both to tell Father Abel. He was so serious and insistent that I could not say no.

At Father Abel's office Larry told the priest, "I want you to witness and bless our engagement." Then he put an ankh ring on my finger. The ankh, a cross with a loop at the top, is an Egyptian symbol of life. Larry told Father Abel that as soon as he arrived in the United States, he was going to work for my visa.

Afterward we attended the Saturday Anticipatory Mass. Before the Mass started, the head of the parish council announced our engagement. The following day Larry and I went to shop for our wedding rings, but we were not successful because we found out all the gold jewelry stores were owned by Orthodox Christians, who didn't do business on Sundays. So Larry brought me to a silversmith to get our ring sizes. Because Larry was leaving the next day, he gave me money for the goldsmith.

The last thing we did before Larry left was to apply for a marriage permit at the Philippine Embassy. It would take time to process because the papers had to be sent to the Ministry of Foreign Affairs in Manila to get my parents' consent and have their signatures authenticated before the papers were returned to the Philippine Embassy in Egypt.

Not long after Larry left, Paulo, the Filipino diplomat I turned down, found out that Larry and I had filed for a marriage permit. He confronted me in the social hall of the embassy, looked at me bitterly, and asked, "Why now are you getting married? You told me you weren't interested to be involved with any man."

He was right. I was shocked and speechless. Paulo was a great catch for most women, including me. But I felt bound to keep my commitment to Larry because I consented in front of Father Abel. When I didn't say anything, Paolo said, "I will just go back to the Philippines for good."

Every single woman at the embassy had a crush on Paulo. He was handsome, highly educated, and very kind. Two weeks after I sought refuge at the Philippine Embassy—after one of the refugees attempted to stab me—he invited me to stay in his apartment. So that I would agree, he said we would not be alone because he had a maid. Paulo treated me like his younger sister. He was truly kind, solicitous, and very respectful. I stayed in his apartment for three weeks, until I found a job and could afford a flat. Later on, his sisterly regard for me changed, forcing me to keep my distance. ✞

13
Waiting for the Fiancée Visa

A week after Larry left for the States, I began wondering if I was doing the right thing in marrying him. I went to confession and told Father Alberto that I was sorry for agreeing to be engaged to Larry and didn't have any intention to fulfill my promise. I wanted to break the engagement and continue with my plan to live and work in Canada.

Father Alberto was all for my marrying Larry. He said Larry is a very good man and God was giving me a gift of the right partner in life. And then I remembered all my prayers asking God to give me a man who acted like a priest. God used Father Alberto to tell me what I needed to hear.

Three weeks had passed since Larry left, without any news from him. So I decided to write him a letter telling him that if he had changed his mind, it was fine with me. I would be all right. I sent the letter to his father's address and hoped his reply would be, "Yes, I am withdrawing our engagement." Instead he wrote back saying he had applied for my fiancée visa and that he would call me.

Larry called three times. Each time I refused to talk to him. My flatmate told me what I was doing was not right because Larry is a good man. So, on his fourth call, I answered the phone. When Larry heard my voice, he started to cry. He asked me why I did not return his calls. I told him I wasn't sure about marrying him. "You know I have two kids in the Philippines," I said.

"All I want to know is whether you are legally married," he answered.

I said, "No."

"Then it's OK," Larry said. Surely I didn't deserve Larry's love.

He told me to cancel my application to go to Canada because he was already filling out the visa papers. I called my friend in Canada who was helping me process my papers and told her I was backing out. She was very disappointed because she had already found a job for me.

✠

Larry applied for my fiancée visa in June 1995. As we waited for the visa to be approved, we wrote each other regularly and talked on the phone every Sunday. I continued to work for the German consul. I also did not neglect my secretarial duties with the Filipino community as well as my church leadership activities.

I occasionally visited the Comboni priests and shared meals with them. I cooked *pansit* (Filipino noodles) for them. I found a new friend in Sister Christina, who worked with the Comboni priests. Occasionally the nun came to the embassy with Father Jose to attend a Filipino function and to sing with me in the choir during Mass.

Sister Christina knew our problem with the visa and prayed that it would be approved soon. It didn't happen. Months passed and I started to worry because my resident visa in Egypt was going to expire in two months. Life became even harder when I found out that some Filipinas were spreading rumors about me. They had seen me in the company of different men, not aware that these were the Comboni priests I brought to the embassy to say Mass.

The rumors reached Larry's boss at the Naval Medical Research Unit (NAMRU) in Egypt. He called Larry's commander in the States, telling him to warn Larry about me. When the commander told Larry I was being unfaithful, Larry said it was not true. He defended me and said I am the kind of woman he loves and trusts. It was a good thing for me that Larry had met these priests. Once, we even went to their rectory, where they served us lunch. Larry's belief in my innocence did not stop the rumors from reaching the American Embassy. I think this further delayed approval of my visa.

I told Father Jose, my spiritual adviser after Father Jim left, that I was going to Israel to make a second pilgrimage. I left for Israel on December 7, 1995, the day before the feast of the Immaculate Conception, and asked the Blessed Virgin for guidance.

After much prayer, I knew what I was going to do. In mid-January 1996, I called Larry. Visa or no visa, I gave him an ultimatum: If he still wanted to marry me, he had to come to Egypt in one week. If he didn't arrive by the seventh day, I would go to Israel on the eighth day. Father Jose kept on telling me we were undergoing a trial. He said it was better for us to be experiencing the trial before rather than after we were married, and then end up divorcing each other.

Larry immediately applied for a leave of absence from his job and called me to say he was arriving January 29 and we were going to get married on February 1. First I bought a wedding gown. Then I asked the administrative officer of the Philippine Embassy to issue me the clearance to get married. He adamantly refused. He said the rule was that marriage plans needed to be posted at the embassy for at least three months before the clearance could be issued. The embassy needed all that time to make sure the applicants were free to get married. So I went up to Ambassador Galenzoga to plead my case. He gave me the clearance right away, saying I deserved it.

The night before Larry flew to Maadi, he called Father Abel to tell him we were going to hold our wedding reception on the church grounds. Father Abel passed the message to me. I had exactly one day to send out invitations and prepare the wedding feast with a friend's help. As soon as Larry arrived, we went to NAMRU to invite Larry's commander. We also invited some of our friends from the American and German embassies; my adopted parents; the entire Philippine Embassy staff, including the ambassador and his wife; and my employer, the consul of the German Embassy. ✠

14
Wedding Day

After Mass on the morning of our wedding, Larry and I went to NAMRU to process the papers we needed. I waited in the office of John, who enumerated all of Larry's faults and tried to convince me not to marry him. I just smiled.

The wedding was scheduled for 4 p.m. At 2 p.m. Larry and I were still cleaning the statue of the Blessed Mother as well as sweeping the churchyard. At 3:30 p.m. Larry's friend Adam arrived to help Larry tape his pant legs up because they were too long. He had bought his suit without fitting it to please me. I had mentioned that in the Philippines, the tradition is not to wear one's wedding clothes until the day of the wedding.

Larry, his friend Adam, and his best man, Robert Naglic, arrived in church before 4 p.m. So did my flatmates and my adopted parents. However, I was still in my boarding house because the person assigned to bring me to church at 3:30 p.m. had not arrived. I could have called a taxi, but as I waited, the negative stuff John had told me about Larry entered my mind and doubts began to creep in that I might be marrying the wrong guy.

I was tempted to remove my wedding dress and not show up in church. Instead I turned to God and asked Him to decide what was best for me. As soon as I was done praying, I heard a knock. Edith, one of our wedding sponsors, was there to pick me up. She rushed me to church, saying that everybody was already there.

Everybody, that is, except my three bridesmaids. They got caught in heavy traffic and showed up 30 minutes after the wedding was over. They had forgotten it was Ramadan and people were rushing home to cook and break their fast at sundown. I ended up getting one of my guests to act as my bridesmaid. It's just too bad because my bridesmaids— my best friend and her two sisters—were beautifully dressed in Christian Dior outfits they had bought in France.

Fathers Jose and Abel officiated at our wedding, which was a mix of American and Filipino traditions. At the reception, we followed the Filipino tradition of releasing two doves while a bell was rung. One of the doves didn't fly high enough and landed on the head of Larry's commander, causing a bit of an injury. We spent our wedding night at the Pullman Hotel overlooking the Nile River. The next day we joined a pilgrimage sponsored by Holy Family Church and visited several Orthodox and Coptic churches.

Larry stayed in my boarding house before he went back to America two weeks later, on St. Valentine's Day. Both of us were crying as we said goodbye because we weren't sure when we would be together again.

The fiancée visa that Larry had applied for eight months earlier was nowhere near being approved, so we tried another approach. Now that we were married, we immediately applied for a relative visa at the U.S. Embassy in Egypt. Sister Christina happened to be a friend of the embassy's newly appointed consul, so we asked her to introduce us. My Egyptian visa was going to expire in July 1996. During the five months before it expired, I followed up on my application at the U.S. Embassy at least three times a week. The answer I always got was, "No result yet."

I was aware that some Filipinos in the community were hoping I wouldn't get my visa until they could find somebody to replace me in my position as their Filipino minister. I also led the Filipino choirs at Holy Family Church and the Philippine Embassy and needed someone to take my place there as well. I prayed hard, begging Jesus and the Blessed

Mother to send somebody soon so that I could join my husband in America.

Again God answered my prayers at the right time. The administrative officer of the Philippine Embassy in Russia was transferred to Egypt and arrived in Holy Week. His wife had a very nice voice and was willing to be soloist at Holy Family. I helped her prepare a mix of English and Filipino songs for the Mass at Holy Family Church as well as at the Philippine Embassy. Her name was also Linda. Was this a coincidence or was it really God's plan to replace me with another Linda? To avoid confusion, we told people to call me Linda 1 and her Linda 2.

There were times when Linda 2 could not sing at Holy Family, so I ended up as soloist, singing mostly Filipino songs. It was OK with the American community, provided I also sang their favorite hymn, "Precious Lord!" I am not a trained singer, but I guess if you are singing for God you will do it well. Many times I had a cold and a sore throat the day before Mass. Amazingly, the following day at Mass my cold was gone.

Linda 2 sang, but God still had to send us someone to take my place as choir leader. Soon a new face appeared at Holy Family. He had just arrived from the States to work for one of the American companies in Egypt. He looked for me and asked if he could play the guitar during Mass. I said yes right away. He also said that he and his family, including his sister who is a nun, led the choir in their parish church in America. Talk of answered prayer!

So now I could leave without feeling guilty. I had already told the congregation that I was staying in Egypt only until the end of June because my residence visa would expire in the first week of July. If I didn't get my relative visa before then, my plan was to go home to the Philippines to visit my children or to wait it out in Israel.

As a parting gift, Father Abel and Frank, the chairman of the parish council, gave me a nice painting of the Holy Family. They handed it to me in front of the congregation after the blessings of the Mass and said they were grateful for all the things I had done for the church. I was so happy because I had really wanted to buy the painting. I didn't expect they would give it to me. This was the icon that I'd been praying to for almost two weeks since returning from my pilgrimage to Israel. It took the place of my Lady of Fatima statue that I bought in Israel, which was then being brought from Filipino home to Filipino home in "block rosary" style, a devotion to the Blessed Virgin that we have in the Philippines. A family prays the rosary daily in front of the Fatima statue. After one week, the family brings the statue in a procession to the next house on the block. Each of the host families serves food as part of their thanksgiving in anticipation of answered prayer.

On June 27 I went to the American Embassy to tell them I was going home and to request transfer of my papers to their embassy in my country. Before I even opened my mouth, the officer asked me if I had $150.

I answered, "No. Why should I give you money and you don't give me my visa?"

The officer said, "That's the reason. You are going to pay for your visa."

Excitedly I went to my friend Mariafe, who kept my money, and told her my visa had been approved. But I asked her to keep it a secret until she bought my plane ticket. I was afraid the people who seemed to enjoy making trouble for me would do something to block me from going to America.

After paying for my visa, I went to St. Joseph Church in Zamalek to offer a thanksgiving Mass. I found I couldn't because the Mass for the day had already been designated for Sister Christina. It was her anniversary Mass. So I took off my gold ring, wrapped it in an Egyptian bill, and dropped it in the offering box. I went to Sister Christina after her special Mass to tell her I'd gotten my visa that morning. She laughed and said her prayer intention for her anniversary Mass was that I would get my visa. Apparently the nuns in Sister Christina's congregation celebrate yearly anniversary

Masses, where they are allowed to pray for one intention. Sister Christina was sure God would answer her prayer for my visa just as He always answered her anniversary prayer request each year.

I spent my remaining days in Egypt on a pilgrimage to St. Ann Damian Monastery, where the body of this special saint of the Egyptian Orthodox Church is buried. It is said that St. Ann's body is incorruptible and that her hands continue producing oil that believers use for healing. I was able to get a small bottle of this oil, which I intended to bring with me to America.

My choir members and the parish council were disappointed when I told them I was leaving on July 4, America's Independence Day, but they wished me well. On July 3 the Comboni priests gave me a farewell party to which my friend Mariafe and the Philippine Embassy staff came to bid me bon voyage. Then, early the next morning, I flew to reunite with my husband and start a new life in America. ☩

Santo Niño

Linda arrives in Kuwait

Linda at desk in Philippine
Embassy, Cairo

Linda at Giza, Egypt, with other Filipina
workers from Kuwait, before her escape

The well of Moses, also
known as the well of Jethro
in Exodus 2:15–21

Remnant of the burning
bush at St. Catherine's
Monastery

Linda and friend on top of Mount Sinai
with the Philippine flag

Linda with Coptic monk at
St. Bishoy Monastery in the
Wadi el-Natrun of Egypt

Fr. Abel and Orthodox Bishop in Holy
Family Church garden, Maadi

FILCOM 94 farewell party for Fr. Jim;
Ling Hicks with Linda and Fr. Jim

FILCOM Cairo officer induction

From left: Fr. Pio, Sr. Christina, Linda, and Fr. Jose

Spot of the Nativity,
Bethlehem

Our Lady of Sorrows,
Church of the Holy
Sepulcher, Jerusalem

Golgatha, the place of the Crucifixion

Linda at Tel Aviv

Linda with Fr. Alberto
(Comboni priest) at the
Philippine Embassy
social hall after Mass,
Cairo, Egypt

Larry in Egypt

Fr. Abel officiating at Linda and Larry's wedding,
February 1,1996

The wedding party, Holy Family Church, Maadi

Mariam's tree near Ein Shams (Old Heliopolis); on their journey to escape Herod, the Holy Family found shade under this sycamore tree; a Chrism is prepared from its oil

PART THREE

15
Coming to America

I arrived at John F. Kennedy airport at 5 a.m. on July 4, 1996. Larry was nowhere around to greet me. I expected him to be there because during our last telephone conversation in Egypt, he said he would arrive before my plane landed. I waited for almost an hour before a Filipina airport employee noticed me and asked if I was waiting for someone. I told her I was newly married and waiting for my husband to pick me up. She thought aloud, "Maybe you are being abandoned."

I did not believe Larry would abandon me, but I got scared anyway. Mrs. Ling Hicks was the only one I knew in the States. As I was looking in my address book for her phone number, Larry showed up. He looked very relieved. He said he'd been waiting for me for a long time. Then he'd finally gone over to the information desk and found me sitting on a bench near it.

Apparently he was waiting for me at another gate. My feelings at that time were a mixture of anger and relief. I wasn't too excited to see him again because even at that time I wasn't so sure this was what I really wanted. I feared we would face problems. To calm myself, I recalled a dream I had when I was in fourth-year high. I dreamt there was a tall, white man waiting for me. He was dressed all in blue. And here was Larry, tall and white, wearing the same blue outfit I saw in that dream.

Larry brought me, his immigrant wife, to Ellis Island as well as to the Statue of Liberty. I could see he was pretty excited to see me. We then drove to his apartment in Gaithersburg, Maryland. The following day Larry brought me to his office and introduced me to his commander and his other officemates. That same week, Nancy, one of Larry's sisters, came to see me. I appreciated her visit very much.

We then drove from Maryland to Windber, Pennsylvania, to visit Larry's father, siblings, and other relatives. On our way to that central part of Pennsylvania, we saw a rainbow. It stayed in the sky all the way to his hometown. Again this rainbow, the mountain, and the big trees on it were exactly as I'd seen it before in my dreams.

It was hardly a year since I was in the process of working for my visa to Canada. I already had a heads-up of where I was going, as God usually gives me a dream or a vision about the next phase in my life. Then he brought me Larry. But I was too hardheaded, too prejudiced about men who weren't priests, that I didn't see Larry was God's answer to my prayers. So I never expected to be viewing Pennsylvania.

✟

We spent our first years of marriage in Gaithersburg. Larry introduced me to Father Filardi and members of St. Martin Church, his parish. I met members of the Legion of Mary, the Marian Cenacle prayer group, and Larry's Bible study group. We ended up becoming members of the Cenacle prayer group and continue to be members to this day, even though we now live in Ephrata, Pennsylvania.

We were also active members of the Legion of Mary, where Larry was the secretary. As active members, we introduced the Philippine block rosary devotion. We led the opening and the closing prayers in each house. Some of the families who accepted the statue of the Blessed Virgin were new to Catholicism and had never prayed the rosary before. We taught them. We also visited some nursing homes just to pray with the patients. If they asked us to pray over them, we did so.

The first time we slept in the home of Larry's father, I dreamt about his mom. She was young, beautiful, had wavy hair, and she was smiling at me. Beside her was Larry's dead brother, Jerry. He had hairy arms and was wearing a red plaid shirt. The next morning I told Larry I dreamt of his mother and brother. He showed me his mom's picture. She looked exactly like she appeared in my dream. As for Jerry's plaid shirt, it hung in the closet where we slept that night. I was certain they'd actually visited me and that made me a bit scared. The following night, when I was by myself in the room, I talked to them like they were actually alive. I said, "I appreciate that you came to visit me even though you are already spirits. But I beg you not to visit me anymore because you belong to another phase of life and I am scared."

I didn't dream about them again until 2004, the year Larry's father died. Then, in 2005, I dreamt of Larry's parents. They were living in a small house and were very happy. In the dream, they were newly married. The dream assured me that Larry's father was in a good place. I had prayed for Larry's father because he was a Protestant and I never saw him going to church. My dream confirmed he is in God's hands because Larry's mother was a very devout Catholic. Larry's extended family is considered to be an ideal family. They have close family ties, which is not typical of all American families.

✢

Almost every time Larry and I traveled to Pennsylvania, we saw a rainbow. Was this just coincidence? But I know God sent a rainbow to Noah as an affirmation that his prayers to stop the rains had been answered. So I believe God was telling me that finally I had reached the place where He had plans for me.

The most amazing rainbow experience for us occurred the day before my birthday in 1996. It was October 23 and Larry was driving me to a train hotel in Strasburg, Pennsylvania. As soon as we left our apartment in Gaithersburg, a rainbow appeared in the sky. Larry and I decided to follow it to where it ended. The rainbow disappeared just when we reached St. Joseph Church in Emmitsburg, the last town in Maryland before crossing over to Pennsylvania. This church had an active visionary. So we stopped and went to a religious gift shop, where Larry bought me my birthday gift. It was a Bible, specifically the St. Joseph Catholic Family edition, because he said St. Joseph was the one who inspired him to marry me. Larry told me he was doing as his father did: The first gift his father gave his mother was a Bible.

When we reached our destination in Strasburg, we attended Saturday Anticipatory Mass at St. Anthony Church, with Father James Small officiating. Afterward we asked him to bless the Bible Larry bought me. We also asked him to write his name on the first page. The world is small, as the saying goes, because seven years later, when we settled into our present home in Ephrata and became members of Our Mother of Perpetual Help (OMPH) Parish, we found Father Small was one of the priests there. He was the one who blessed our present home as well.

One week after my birthday, Larry and I joined a three-day retreat sponsored by the Legion of Mary. We slept in separate rooms. This gave me a chance to seriously meditate about what God wanted me to do. But first he wanted me to be at peace with all the people who had harmed me, as well as with people whose feelings I had hurt. So I sent early Christmas cards not only to my friends but also to people I disliked.

After the retreat, Larry was assigned to the USNS Comfort (T-AH 20), a hospital ship berthed in Baltimore. While he was away I experienced stomach pains. I thought they were premenstrual cramps, so when Larry returned from duty, I told him to buy Midol to ease my discomfort. Larry looked at me thoughtfully. He then asked me to give him a sample of my urine. Later he called saying he wasn't buying Midol. He said in a very excited voice, "You're pregnant."

It was December 13, 1996, and God had answered Larry's prayer. Apparently he had been praying daily for a child, aware that he was 43 and I was 37 when we married. Immediately I knew this was the reward God had promised me while I meditated at the Legion of Mary retreat. ✞

16
Pregnancy

During my pregnancy, I had a craving for mango. I awoke Larry at midnight to buy me a mango even though he was very sleepy. He found it difficult to understand my unreasonable demands. As a Filipino, I love rice, but during the early stages of my pregnancy I could not stand the smell of cooked rice. All I wanted to eat was spaghetti and pizza—foods I never liked before—and mango.

These were the early years of our marriage and the adjusting period was not easy. I admit I was more difficult than usual, which is saying a lot. Then there were the many cultural differences to hurdle. But God always helped smooth out our differences. Both of us recognized that our union is sacred and God wants us to be together. It might not have been our choice in the beginning, but we recognized that God put us together in an unusual manner.

✠

The night before we went to Baltimore to attend a Valentine's Day party at Mrs. Ling Hicks' church, I dreamt I was dancing with a woman with a tan complexion. I can hardly describe how beautiful she was, and what a good dancer. Anyhow, I was two months pregnant, but that did not hinder me from dancing well with Mrs. Hicks at the party. Later, on my way to the restroom, I touched the statue of St. Therese of the Little Flower. I noticed that she looked like the woman I was dancing with in my dream. Later that night, my raffle ticket won me a basket of flowers. So, I added St. Therese of the Little Flower to my short list of favorite saints. The list includes St. Teresa of Jesus (also known as St. Teresa of Avila). Later, when we moved to Lancaster, I added St. Pio to the list.

In the beginning of my pregnancy, we became members of Couples for Christ. This is a Catholic group that involves everybody—from married couples to Kids for Christ and Servants of Christ for the single and the widowed. Besides going to Mass on Sundays, we met every Friday night with different couples. We began with an opening song followed by a prayer for our intentions. Then the husbands talked with each other and the wives talked to other wives, discussing ways to improve their marriage relationships.

To be a member of this group, we were obliged to attend a Marriage Enrichment training program offered by the leader of the group. We were fortunate that our leader was an expert marriage counselor from the Philippines. From him we learned many practices. To this day, part of our commitment is to say opening and closing prayers with our weekend meals, wherein we thank God for all the blessings we received during the week. Also, at least two times a month, we say an opening prayer before holding a one-on-one conversation. We talk about the good things we have done as well as any problems and disagreements—and we try to resolve them. In addition, we discuss our future plans. We write all this in our personal journals.

We named our daughter Maryann—a combination of the Blessed Mother's name and St. Ann. She was born on July 29, 1997, at the Naval Hospital in Bethesda, Maryland. The day I delivered Maryann, Larry's commander and his office-mates visited me in my room while our beautiful baby girl contentedly slept beside me. Three days later, we went home to our apartment in Gaithersburg, where some members of Couples for Christ, the Legion of Mary, and the Cenacle prayer group visited Maryann and me.

Since I wasn't working, I went to Mass every day. So three days after she was born, Maryann was already attending daily Mass. When we moved to Ephrata and I became a substitute teacher, it became impossible for me to go to Mass on the days I needed to be at school very early. But Maryann continued to attend Mass daily until she graduated from OMPH school. I dropped her off at OMPH Church. Then, after Mass, she walked to her classroom, which is located in a building attached to the church.

Maryann was baptized in Windber, where the majority of Larry's relatives live, 12 days after she was born. Larry's father seemed happy to see his granddaughter. Larry's sister Bernadette and her husband, Steve, were the godparents. Maryann didn't cry when the priest poured water on her head. She was probably tired since she had been crying all day before her christening. The food we served afterward was a combination of Filipino and American dishes.

One of Maryann's eyes kept on tearing up and crusting. I had to wipe that eye almost every minute. At the Naval Hospital we were told the eye was plugged. They scheduled her to have eye surgery when she was 6 months old. I often prayed for healing for other people. Many of them returned to me saying they were healed. This time I prayed for my daughter's healing.

A week before the designated date for Maryann's surgery, I noticed her eye had stopped tearing. I thanked God for listening to my prayers. However, we kept Maryann's appointment. The doctor examined her and said she was OK. She didn't need to undergo surgery. He asked me what had happened. I simply told him that I had prayed to God for her healing and my prayers were answered.

When Maryann was 9 months old, Larry was deployed to the Baltic Sea as part of his tour of duty in the Navy. He was to stay there for six months, which meant Larry wouldn't be present for his daughter's first birthday. He was sad and frustrated.

As soon as he left, I started a novena to Our Lady of Antipolo, the Philippine patron saint of travelers. I trusted the Virgin to protect him from any harm and bring him safely back to us. But I also made the novena because I was still new to life in America and I was a bit scared to be left alone at night in our apartment. So I made night as my day and stayed up till 3 or 4 a.m. But I still got up before 8 a.m. in order to attend Mass at St. Martin's. I pushed Maryann's stroller to church, a good 30-minute walk away. This was my exercise as well as my time to do some errands. But I was thankful whenever our neighbor, a Korean lady, gave us a ride in her car.

My prayer life remained intense even though I was taking care of a newborn. Each day I prayed the glorious, joyful, and sorrowful mysteries of the rosary, a practice I picked up in Egypt from my priest friends. I did this because, like St. Theresa of Avila, I wanted to experience what the priests and monks told me: If you are in a state of grace, the Holy Spirit will give you peace of mind and contentment despite the difficulties that may come your way. God will always be there to lift you up. I recited my prayer to St. Brigit, as well as my novenas to St. Therese, the Little Flower, and St. Jude.

I also continued the religious practices of fasting I learned from Father Abel and other priest friends. Each Wednesday and Friday I fasted and abstained from eating meat and any dish containing milk and eggs. Each first Wednesday of the month I ate just bread in honor of the Blessed Mother. Each First Friday I drank only water during the day and broke my fast at midnight.

I also rigidly fasted during Holy Week to be in union with Christ's Passion and for the conversion of sinners. Whenever I fasted in Egypt, I remember, I smelled fragrant flowers. Even the friend who went with me one Holy Week to St. Sergius Church (built on the spot where the Holy Family hid during their flight to Egypt) told me she smelled flowers. She said she smelled them only when we were together in a taxi. That's when I knew the Holy Spirit was with us.

To this day I don't eat meat on Wednesdays and Fridays, a practice that my husband and daughter also have adopted. I still don't eat any meat during Lent, but now I eat dairy products. Occasionally I choose not to go to work, eat bread once a day, and set aside that day for prayer in front of the tabernacle. I believe we have to work for temporal things like food to feed our bodies. But we also need to set aside time to nourish our souls through prayer.

✠

When Larry was away from us, I put Maryann in a play area in our living room. I barricaded the area with a 1-foot fence that I propped up with pillows. She played inside this safe area while I prayed inside our bedroom for at least an hour. That was my daily routine after we came back from church.

One day I was only 15 minutes into my prayer when I felt very hungry. I stopped praying and went to the kitchen to eat something. I looked toward Maryann's play area and gasped. Maryann wasn't in the play area but on top of the table. She was pointing to the crucifix hanging above the table and saying "Jesus! Jesus!" At that age she could only say "Mom" and "Dad." How was she able to climb the 3-foot-high table? To this day, I don't know the answer.

Months before Maryann's birthday I started cooking food for a big celebration. I put the food in the freezer and sent early invitations to our co-parishioners. Someone suggested I should celebrate Maryann's birthday only after Larry arrived. I told them, "Larry will be here on Maryann's birthday." Another one asked how I knew that. I replied, "I'm praying for it." I didn't tell them I was praying continuous novenas to Our Lady of Antipolo.

The majority of people I invited responded to my RSVP to come to Maryann's birthday with or without Larry's presence. The night before Maryann's birthday I went to bed at 7 p.m. As soon as I lay down I smelled Larry's scent. It was how he smelled coming back from work—a mix of his aftershave lotion and sweat. I took that as a sign from God that he would be at Maryann's birthday. I had hardly slept when the phone rang. It was Larry. He said he had just arrived at the Naval Hospital in Bethesda and was coming home in 20 minutes.

He was coming earlier than he'd expected because a Navy officer canceled his trip home by plane, and Larry's name was pulled up to take his place on the plane for VIPs. Otherwise, Larry was set to go home by ship together with the other Navy men. That would have been a two-month trip home. So, Our Lady of Antipolo answered my prayers. And the following day, Maryann's birthday, everybody was surprised to see Larry there. ☦

17
Larry Retires from the Navy

Larry retired from the Navy in October 1998. In December we moved to Windber so that his relatives could help in case we needed a babysitter for Maryann.

However, we had to compete with my sister-in-law who had a small child and also expected help. Larry's relatives as well as Larry and I are devout Catholics, but that did not stop us from having conflicts. There was pressure dealing with in-laws, and Larry always took the side of his relatives over me. We were undergoing a difficult trial in our marriage.

But we still attended Mass every day and continued with our prayer devotions. We attended either an 8 a.m. Mass in Windber or a noon Mass in Altoona. We also went to the Cathedral in Altoona for confession each first Saturday in honor of the Blessed Mother.

Before Bishop James John Hogan died in 2005, I had the chance to confess my sins to him. My usual manner of confessing is to tell the priest all the sins I committed in the past, emphasizing my life with Rolly and my leaving the children, because I wasn't sure if I was totally forgiven. Bishop Hogan seemed to read my mind because he told me he knew I prayed a lot for myself and for others. Then he said that as a bishop he had the power to absolve me of all the mortal and venial sins I had committed since I was young. He also asked me to pray for him. So from then on I had real peace of mind that God forgave me for all the sins I committed in the past.

One night I dreamt of Jesus. He was wearing a white cloth around the lower part of His body. He was the most handsome man I'd ever seen. He looked at me and I could see the goodness and sincerity in his eyes. Someone in my dream told me to shake His hands, but I hesitated because I was not worthy to be close to Him. He continued to look at me. When I didn't make any move to go to Him, He came and hugged me. I woke up startled. Larry and I were undergoing trial in our marriage. For me, this dream was proof that Jesus was always there to console, assist, and give me the grace to endure.

Meanwhile, Larry continued to apply for jobs in Windber, but nothing came of it.

I eased my boredom by learning to drive in preparation for the time I would begin to hold a job of my own. We went to different sites of devotion in Pennsylvania, and went twice to the Church of St. Anthony in Pittsburgh. This church has several relics of different saints. I prayed for two things: that we would be able to take a vacation in the Philippines to see my children and my parents, and that when we got back, Larry would be offered a good job. ✟

18
Larry Lands a Job

On the day of our flight to visit Jerilyn, Jerry, and the rest of my family in the Philippines, the three of us were sick and taking antibiotics. We decided to go to the island of Cebu in central Philippines instead of to my family in Cagayan so we wouldn't spread our sickness to them. The highlight of our trip to Cebu was a visit to the Shrine of the Santo Niño located on the beach in Mactan, which was only a 45-minute drive from our hotel. The Santo Niño is Cebu's patron saint. The original statue, which is believed to have been brought by Ferdinand Magellan when he came to the islands in 1521 to convert the natives, is enshrined in Mactan. Devotees claim it has miraculous powers. We went there on a First Friday and the Basilica Minore del Santo Niño was packed. We inched our way to the altar, lit a candle, and then prayed that by the time we returned to the States, Larry would have a job waiting for him. After four days we flew back to Manila, from where we took another plane headed for Tuguegarao.

I hadn't seen my children in 10 years and was excited to see them. I'd completely missed out on their childhood. Jerilyn was now 12 and Jerry, 10. I understood why my daughter was closer to my parents than to me. But Jerry was different. He actually slept on the floor mat with me and Maryann, while Larry slept alone on the bed.

Jerry had just completed the third grade and Jerilyn, the sixth grade. She graduated with second honors, which should have satisfied her, but she had topped her class from grades 1 to 5. Her reason for "not doing well" was her teeth. For several months she complained of a terrible toothache, but my parents did not have the extra money to bring her to a dentist. Jerilyn said she prayed for me to visit so I could do something about it.

We stayed in Maconacon for just one week. Then we went to Tuguegarao so Jerilyn could get dental treatment. The dentist said she had a tooth abscess, one that could have led to her death if left untreated. This was the first time Jerilyn left the safety of Maconacon. My parents never brought my children outside the small town my father founded when I was small because they feared Rolly would kidnap them. Rolly had also warned my parents that if they allowed me to bring "his kids" to the States, they would receive a "big prize" from him. So my parents kept Jerilyn and Jerry in Maconacon until they both finished high school.

When Jerilyn was in nursing school, she wrote me that she wanted to see her father in Manila. I consented. I told my parents to bring both children to see their father because they were old enough to understand the reason I left. Jerilyn wrote me afterward. She said the visit made her realize how irresponsible her father was. Larry helped me finance her studies in nursing, for which Jerilyn was grateful. And after she got married, she wrote me to say that she respected Larry more than ever.

By the time Jerry was ready for college, I was earning enough to be able to support his course in computer programming without Larry's help. Today, my children are both able to support themselves. However, I still send money home to help augment their small salaries. I also help my father as well as my orphaned niece who is now in high school.

✝

When we returned to Windber, I began studying for my citizenship exams and Larry continued looking for a job. Two months passed by and we started getting desperate because Larry was still jobless. Then one night in early May, I dreamt I was under a big tree filled with white flowers. A lady all in white approached me, took a flower from the tree, and gave it to me. I smelled the flower. Its scent was fresh and wonderful, but I could not identify what flower it was. When I woke up, I knew right away the lady was Our Lady of Fatima. I also knew she wanted us to make a novena to her because May is the month when she appeared to the three children in Fatima.

I told Larry about the dream and that we needed to find the flower the Lady gave me. We would place it on our altar and then start our novena. I told Larry I interpreted the dream as a sign from the Blessed Mother that he would get the job after we finished the novena.

We went to different flower shops for white flowers. They didn't smell like the one in my dream. Then, while shopping in a Giant supermarket in Windber, we found it. The clerk said the flowers came from Germany and that they were mistakenly delivered to them. We placed the flowers on our altar and started our novena. A week after we finished the novena, Larry was offered a job interview by the Pennsylvania Department of Health in Exton. Three days later he received another invitation from an office in Harrisburg.

The Exton opening was for an inspector, a position Larry had never held before. He was scared to take it. Larry preferred the Harrisburg job because the work he would do there was almost aligned with his degree as a microbiologist. His father, brothers, and sisters agreed he should interview for the second job. But I encouraged him to go for the Exton job, for the most important reason: It came first after we finished our novena. Therefore it was the answer to our prayer. I told him not to be afraid. The Blessed Virgin would be with him. Larry trusted me and decided to go for the Exton job. He went for his initial interview the last week in June and found he had a lot of competition. Our faith was being tested because three months passed with no word from the company.

Meanwhile, I took the citizenship exam in Johnstown, passed it, and was told I would be sworn in on October 13, 2000. I took note of the day and was comforted because the 13th day of the month is special to Our Lady of Fatima.

Then Larry was called for a second interview in the last week of September. When he returned home, he was beaming. "I got the job," he told me. He was supposed to start in the first week of October but he asked to start after my swearing in as an American citizen. ✟

19
New Town, New Life

We chose to move to Lancaster County instead of Chester County, where Exton is located. Larry found an apartment in New Holland, 25 miles west of Exton. While I stayed behind to pack, Larry went ahead to live in the apartment. The apartment was close to Our Lady of Lourdes Catholic Church, and I looked forward to being active in the parish. I joined their Bible study and had a chance to tell them about my experiences climbing Mount Sinai three times and my three pilgrimages to the Holy Land.

Our Lady of Lourdes offered Mass on Sundays, on weekdays, and on the first Saturday of each month. So, on the three Saturdays when the church didn't offer Mass, we attended Mass at Our Mother of Perpetual Help Church in the neighboring town of Ephrata. We joined their Cenacle prayer group that met after the 9 a.m. Saturday Mass.

One time I attended a healing service at Lourdes Church. Many of us were stricken by the Holy Spirit and fell to the floor. Unfortunately I landed on the chest of a woman who walked with the aid of a cane. She screamed for help because she couldn't breathe. They called a paramedic and rushed her to the hospital. I got so scared that I did not want to return to the church, even though Larry and I had made some new friends in the parish.

That's how we started going exclusively to OMPH Church. The parish also runs a school, and we were planning ahead for Maryann.

We started looking to buy a home in Ephrata. Larry and I could not seem to agree to buy any of the houses we saw. It was coming almost to a year that we'd been looking and we were not successful.

I was desperate to buy a house and move closer to OMPH Church. So I decided to do something special for the Blessed Mother. I asked Larry to look for somebody who could make a crown for my Fatima statue. Larry found a goldsmith in Richland Township. I gave him many pieces of my most valuable gold jewelry to make the crown. It took the goldsmith almost a month to finish it. A week after I placed the crown on my Fatima statue, we spotted a house for sale on our way home to New Holland from OMPH Church.

Larry called the selling agent to arrange for us to see the house. It was old and needed to be repainted; but as soon as I entered the doorway, I felt at peace. There was a balcony on the second floor landing from where one could look down on the high-ceilinged living room. I loved that feature. There were two fair-sized rooms and one small one on the second floor. It played on my mind right away that we could convert the small room into a chapel to hold our saints. The room remains a chapel to this day. I have invited all my guests—priests, nuns, and laity—to use it when they want to pray.

Our agent quoted a price that Larry was willing to pay, but I told Larry to make a counteroffer for $20,000 less. Our agent said the listing agent would not agree. But amazingly the owner of the house, who lived next door, agreed to our price. I was so grateful that the Blessed Mother helped us buy our house. The former owners still live next door and they are very good people.

We bought the house early in December and moved in on December 21, 2002. However, the blessing of our house was delayed because Larry got very sick from all the stress of moving. It was the first time in our married life that Larry got so sick that he could not stand up. He was seriously ill for a couple of days, so I decided to pray over him. Amazingly, as soon as I finished praying over him, he said he felt healed.

I said, "It's like magic."

But he said, "No, it's your prayers."

The same thing happens with Maryann. She gets sick, I pray over her, and almost instantly she gets better. However, when I am the one who gets sick, I need to go to the doctor for treatment.

Father Small blessed our house on February 1. It was also our wedding anniversary. We renew our vows each year so that God will give us grace to have a good relationship as a couple. So Father Small also presided over our renewal of wedding vows.

Maryann was 5 years old when we moved to Ephrata. She started preschool at OMPH School, which is run by nuns, priests, and lay teachers. Her adjustment to school life was faster and less painful than my adjustment to life in Ephrata. There were a few friendly people in town, but many looked at me as an outsider, which hurt my feelings. I felt discriminated against and cried a couple of times. But then I remembered my uncle's advice when I was a child in the Philippines. He told me to pray for the person who hurt me and be nice in return, because that's what God wants.

At this point Larry was well settled at Exton. He knew everything his new job entailed and was so glad he listened to me. The job utilized what he learned from his degree as well as his experience in the laboratory department at the Naval Hospital in Bethesda. The only part he could have had less of was the traveling. He did a lot of that in the 24 years he was in the Navy. In this new job he had to travel—and he still does to this day—all around the state for the Pennsylvania Department of Health, and around the country for annual training required by the Center for Medicare and Medicaid services. ✞

20
I Land a Job

It took three years before I got my current job as a substitute teacher in the School District of Lancaster. That's because it was so difficult to get my transcript of records and other credentials from the Philippines.

One time I went to St. John Neumann Church in Manheim Township and joined a novena in the saint's honor. There I found out that the saint's body is incorruptible and that he is buried under the altar of St. Peter's Catholic Church in Philadelphia.

It played on my mind that I needed the saint to intercede for me. On the saint's feast day, I begged Larry to bring me to Philadelphia, a 70-mile drive from Ephrata. We attended Mass and joined the procession. I knelt before the incorruptible body of St. John Neumann and prayed that I would get my credentials soon. I told the saint I needed a job that paid more than what I got as a staffer with OMPH's After-School Program. I needed to send money to my children and other relatives in the Philippines. Larry did help once in a while, but on one paycheck it was a struggle to send money home. Also, I felt ashamed to ask my husband for money for my relatives.

Anyhow, the same week we visited St. John Neumann, my brother Victor called to say he got my transcript through the help of the registrar, who happened to be his previous professor. Since that time, I have been a devotee of the saint. Each year we try to attend his anniversary celebration in Philadelphia.

✟

As soon as I got my transcript, I applied right away as a substitute teacher within the Lancaster School District. I submitted my application the week that Pope John Paul II was very ill. I knew he was a living saint, so the morning he died I immediately prayed to him to intercede on my behalf. I prayed for a quick approval because I was told my application would take three months to process.

The day after the pope died, the Substitute Teacher Service of the Lancaster School District called me to teach in one of Lancaster County's city schools. I was very surprised. Did this mean I had been certified without my knowledge? I went on the Internet. Indeed, my certification had been approved the day the pope died. It was less than a week since I submitted my papers.

I continue working as a substitute teacher for two agencies in the City of Lancaster as well as Lancaster County. I always pray to Pope John Paul II to grant me assignments every day, except on first Fridays. But when I encounter difficult students, I pray to St. John Neumann. ♱

21
Finding an Answer Through Dreams

Our Cenacle prayer group meets Saturdays after 9 a.m. Mass in the chapel adjacent to the main sanctuary. We pray the rosary in front of an icon of Our Mother of Perpetual Help. The icon is surrounded by electric candles. But when we first joined the group in 2001, the chapel had no icon. That's why I brought my statue of Our Lady of Fatima. Then I heard that somebody had questioned my motives. I felt bad and cried about it.

I mentioned this to Father Jim. He felt my pain because he knew how much I love the Blessed Mother. However, to avoid criticism, he advised me to stop bringing my personal statue. In its place, I brought a prayer card with a picture of Our Lady of Fatima and looked at it while reciting the rosary. Nobody objected to that.

A few weeks after that incident, I dreamt that our group was praying in front of an icon of the Blessed Mother and the icon was surrounded by wax candles. I mentioned my dream to some people in the group, and they just smiled. Indeed, my dream came true, except for the part about wax candles.

In 2003 I dreamt I was in the field close to OMPH School and saw the Blessed Mother. She was dressed in a long, white silk gown and she was running among the tall grasses and weeds. She saw me and begged me to help her because some kids were throwing stones and mud at her. I woke up and immediately told Larry about the dream. I said there must be a statue of the Blessed Mother in the field because my dream was so real.

Larry dismissed me, saying, "It's just a dream." I found his reaction strange because he knows better than to take my dreams lightly. In the past, when I insisted my dreams were true, he found ways to double check. And he had seen many of my dreams come true.

Later he told me he thought the field in my dream was in the Philippines. That's why he dismissed it. Since I was scared to venture out to the field on my own and didn't know which people to trust in church and in Maryann's school, I ignored the dream, but never really forgot it. I had one close friend, Sister Doris, whom I met when I joined the OMPH choir in 2001. However, when I had this dream, she wasn't around. She had been transferred to Shenandoah Convent in Shenandoah, Pennsylvania.

In the summer of 2004, Sister Doris became our house-guest for three days. I told her about my dream and asked if a statue that resembled the Lady in that dream existed in the field near OMPH School. She said yes. She also said teenagers had vandalized the statue and that some of the statue's fingers were broken. Sister Doris wanted us to go to the field and visit the Virgin. She felt bad that the statue was abandoned. But I said no because of my troubles with my Fatima statue in my Cenacle prayer group.

There was another incident, and it was connected with the first time I taught a religious education class. It was the feast of the Immaculate Conception and I decided to place my Fatima statue on the teacher's table. Before I proceeded to the main topic, I thought it appropriate to say something about why we were celebrating the Immaculate Conception. After the class, I heard that somebody had complained, saying that what I did would chase away the students. So, after a couple of sessions I decided to quit teaching religious education. I did mention the complaint to one of the parish priests. He was upset. Why would anyone prevent me from talking about the Blessed Mother? This became the subject of one of his homilies.

In 2007, some ladies from our church said that while walking through the field they spotted a statue of the Blessed Mother surrounded by tall grasses and weeds. They approached our pastor, the Rev. Patrick McGarrity, who is a devotee of the Blessed Mother, and asked him if they could clean the statue and the grotto. I was so happy when I heard the news that I called one of the ladies and thanked her.

My mistake was that I mentioned my dream of three years earlier. I was told that one of the ladies felt bad because I knew about the statue first, and in a dream at that. My only intention was to thank the ladies and to encourage people to visit the statue and pray to her. Ever since the statue and the grotto were cleaned, Larry and I have been going there to pray at least three times a week. When Sister Doris visited us again one summer, I hosted a party for her and invited one of her friends who had cleaned the grotto. I asked Sister Doris to tell this friend that I did dream about the statue three years before and that I wasn't making up a story.

When we first moved to Lancaster County, I experienced a lot of discrimination. It was most noticeable when I joined a Scrabble tournament held in Lancaster County in July 2002. I joined it because I played Scrabble in the Philippines and once won a school tournament sponsored by my alma mater. However, when I registered, I was asked, "Are you going to play in English?"

I felt like an outsider and didn't do well that first time, winning only one out of seven games. However, in the second tournament I joined, I won 5 of 12 games. I recognize that I would not have won those games without the help of St. Michael, the archangel, whose power is from God.

Early in my marriage I read a book about angels and found out God gave them the power to perform miracles. Before the tournament I didn't really pray to angels. Why should I pray to an angel when I can pray directly to God or the Blessed Mother? (At that time I wasn't even introduced yet to St. Pio and his miraculous powers of healing.)

The night before I went to the tournament, Larry and I discussed angels. Larry is a firm believer in angels. But I told him I would just pray directly to God or to the Blessed Mother. At 3 or 4 a.m. on the day of the tournament, I was awakened by a noise and a feeling that someone was on my left side. Without opening my eyes, I envisioned a big man dressed all in white, his feathered wings flapping. I turned my face toward Larry, who was asleep on my right side. I wanted to tell him there was an angel beside me and, yes, I firmly believe in an angel's power. I didn't have the chance to tell him what happened that night until I came back from the tournament affirming that angels really help.

On the day of the tournament I attended Mass. Then Father Brendan Greany gave me a blessing. He mentioned that I needed to pray to St. Michael for help because it was his feast day. Father Brendan was right. I won five games straight. In one of the games I played an eight-letter word that touched two triple-word squares, for a score of 145 points. Since that experience, I always remember to pray to St. Michael and to my guardian angel.

My husband has a strong influence in my life. I consider him a holy man and sometimes God puts the words in his mouth when I turn to him with my concerns or doubts. One time, on EWTN, the Catholic network, we heard Father Benedict Groeschel talk about his near-death experience. He said that while he was near death, God allowed him to see the reality of hell and purgatory. He also said that even if we die in the state of grace, we need to be purified in purgatory. I told Larry that I disagreed with the priest. What is our incentive to try to be good and follow God's commandments if there is no way our sins will be completely forgiven? I believed that when the priest, who represents God, forgives your sins and gives you absolution and then you die immediately after that, it means you should go directly to heaven. I went to bed at that time feeling discouraged and telling myself that Father Groeschel was mistaken.

Whenever I go to bed with a question or a concern, I often find an answer through my dreams. When I wake up, I am able to interpret what God wants to tell me. That night I dreamt that a very powerful man wanted to take advantage of me. To escape him, I ran all the way to the top of the hill. This hill was very steep, so there was no way for me to survive if I fell. The man followed me all the way to the top and I was trapped. There was no escaping him, so I told myself that God would forgive me if the man succeeded in his bad intentions against me because it would be against my will. Then another man wearing a white robe pushed me down the hill and I died. I could see my spirit lifting out of my body as the man in white told me that he would rather have me die than have me taken advantage of.

Afterward I found myself under the ground. It was very dim. Only one candle lit the place. I saw souls barricaded inside a steel fence. I was outside the fence looking at them. And then I woke up. I realized that God was telling me in that dream that if we committed mortal sin, we would be forgiven through the sacrament of reconciliation. However, when we die, we still need to go through the process of purification, that is, purgatory, before we go to heaven. ♱

22
Devotions and Spiritual Practices

During one of our visits to Sister Doris at Shenandoah Convent, she told me she was working for the canonization of Father Walter J. Ciszek. Born in Shenandoah, the priest was assigned to Russia, where he was sentenced to hard labor in the Gulag. After 30 years, he was released and returned home to the United States.

Father Ciszek had a special devotion to the Blessed Mother. On the feast of her Immaculate Conception, he died while asleep on his chair. I sat on that chair and considered myself very blessed to be sitting on the chair of a holy man who one day may be canonized.

Then Sister Doris told me in a kind voice that I was the first one to sit on that chair after he died because nobody was allowed to sit on it. I quickly stood up, very embarrassed, and apologized. That chair is now on exhibit in the former rectory where Father Ciszek stayed.

Sister Doris showed us a jar filled with notes Father Ciszek wrote when he was still alive. She told me to pick one, saying that whatever note I drew from the jar would have meaning in my life. My note read, "Eucharistic Minister." Sister Doris nodded her head. "You need to discern," she said.

Back home I prayed that if God wanted me to be an extraordinary minister of the Holy Eucharist, more commonly known as Eucharistic minister, He would pave the road for me. I contacted Andy Marvin, the man in charge of extraordinary Eucharistic ministers at OMPH. He said my request was timely because a weekend training seminar for aspiring Eucharistic ministers was going to be held in three days at the Harrisburg Diocese.

I had three days to get a written permission from Father Pat that I needed to submit to the Harrisburg Diocese. The next day, after 9 a.m. Mass, I approached Father Pat. Before I opened my mouth he said, "You want to become a Eucharistic minister." I followed him to his office and he gave me the written permission. Larry drove me to Harrisburg to attend the training. Just as soon as my uniform was finished, OMPH scheduled me to serve in a Mass. To this day I still serve as Eucharistic minister in our church.

As a family, our favorite prayer group is the Legion of Mary because Maryann gets to participate in praying the rosary and making prayer requests. We host the rosary in our house for support of the Legion of Mary. I also host other rosary groups for adults as well as children, but sometimes I mix the adults and children together. We celebrate Christmas at home by praying the rosary with my guests. We also pray the rosary during feast days of the Blessed Mother, as well as the feast day of St. Pio.

In 2006, we invited friends to pray the rosary in honor of Our Lady of Fatima. Our house was packed with about 50 people, including Father Jim and his friends who came from Washington, D.C., to join us in praying the rosary. Larry and I are very grateful to count Father Jim as one of our friends. He also continues to be my spiritual advisor. When he first visited us in the United States, it was near Christmas of 2004, and he celebrated Mass at our house. ✟

23
Holy Love

We have gone on a number of pilgrimages to shrines of the Blessed Mother here in America. We visited the Shrine of the Immaculate Conception in Washington, D.C., where they installed a replica of the statue of Our Lady of Antipolo. We visited Mary's shrine at Emmitsburg, Maryland; the shrine of Our Lady of Consolation in Ohio; and the World Apostolate of Fatima Shrine of the Immaculate Heart of Mary in Washington, New Jersey. We joined Filipinos who celebrated the arrival in New Jersey of a replica of the statue of Our Lady of Piat, my mother's favorite. We also joined a group of Filipinos when they celebrated the anniversary of Our Lady of Barangay, another statue of the Blessed Mother venerated in the Philippines.

But the most significant place we visited was in Holy Love, Ohio, where the Blessed Mother was giving messages to a visionary. Thousands of people have gone there in hopes of witnessing a miracle.

Three months before we visited Holy Love, I dreamt of a statue of the Blessed Mother. She was dressed in beige and she looked entirely different from my other dreams of Mary. In that dream I went to a hill and prayed for a miracle, and my prayers were granted. I mentioned my dream to Larry and said we might be going on a pilgrimage, but I still didn't know where.

A month later, we joined the first Saturday prayer group at the National Centre for Padre Pio in Barto, Pennsylvania. There I heard from a couple about the apparitions in Holy Love. For some reason I felt Holy Love was where I would find the statue I saw in my dream. When I told Larry, he was hesitant to go because the drive would take eight hours. But he knew in his heart that my dream was true.

Finally he decided we would start out on September 14, the day before the feast day of Our Lady of Sorrows, so we could be at Holy Love on September 15. I saw the original statue of Our Lady of Sorrows when I visited Jerusalem for the first time with Father Jim and Daylin. At that time, Father Jim told me to make a special request, and if it was granted, I had to return to give a gift. I prayed to find a good husband I could trust, and I found Larry. After we married in Egypt, I returned to Jerusalem and offered my 21-carat gold ring to Our Lady of Sorrows.

Halfway to Ohio, we stopped and slept over at my sister-in-law's house in Windber. The affirmation to our trip started when we got up in the morning and Audrey offered us tea. She knew I didn't like black tea but thought I might like what she had. When I poured water on the tea, it smelled like a rose. I drank it and really liked it. In Pittsburgh we stopped at an Asian restaurant where Larry usually ate whenever he was on a business trip in that area. Again, there they offered us rose tea.

When we were close to our destination, Larry asked me again to describe the statue that I had dreamt, probably just to test me. I told him she had on a beige dress with gold trim and her face was broader than the faces of Mary in my previous dreams.

The small chapel at Holy Love was filled with people. On the walls were photos taken at the site where Mary gave the messages to the visionary. One of those photos caught my attention. It was a photo of a big cross that appeared in the sky. I had seen the same cross outside our house every night for two weeks when the moon was full. It was a big cross-shaped beam of light coming from the moon, with the center shaft shining on our front yard outside our kitchen window. Father Jim had seen it when he visited us on Maryann's 10th birthday. Because of this, I placed a statue of Mary there. The cross-shaped shaft of light continued to show daily until May 2007, and once a month after that.

✞

My concern was to look for the statue I had seen in my dream. It wasn't in the main area of the chapel where the people were lining up to pray. Where was it? Maybe this time my dream was not true. As I prayed, a bit disappointed, Larry continued looking in every corner of the chapel. There, hidden in one corner, he found a statue that fit my description exactly. He also found a lock of hair inside the glass case that housed the statue. The Blessed Mother gave this relic to the visionary. It was put in a tiny plastic bag and placed there to keep it safe. Only a few people were going there to pray.

We went to our hotel to rest a while before returning at 10 p.m. to join the crowd of devotees in reciting three mysteries of the rosary at the site where the apparition would take place. We put on our rain boots because it was raining very hard. When we arrived at the site, the rain stopped. Maryann and I smelled roses, tea roses. The sky was dark because it had rained. But at midnight, when the Blessed Mother appeared to the visionary, we saw pink clouds on top of white clouds in the sky. Thirty minutes after the message was given, the sky turned dark again and the rain resumed. It rained until we went back to our hotel.

The next day we went back to the site and prayed the rosary to Our Lady of Sorrows, made the Stations of the Cross, and attended the Anticipatory Saturday Mass.

I continued smelling roses all morning. When we returned in the afternoon, I noticed that the altar was fully decorated with big roses. We stayed in the back so nobody would notice us. However, the person in charge of the Mass approached us and asked us to offer the gifts to the altar. They let me hold the host, Maryann held the wine and water, and Larry held the basket. They could have picked someone from the parish to do the honors, not strangers to Holy Love. I thanked God for the privilege of being one of the servers at this special Mass.

✝

The night we arrived home, I noticed that the face of my Fatima statue was pinkish in color. When I was in Egypt, I got visible answers to my prayers in this way. If the Virgin approved, the face of my Fatima statue turned pinkish. If she disapproved, it turned dark. In our home in Ephrata, my Fatima statue's face would turn dark if we didn't pray the rosary during her feast day.

There was one time I cooked a lot of food and invited several guests on the feast of the Immaculate Conception. We didn't pray the rosary because my guests were not Catholic. When the guests left, I looked at my Fatima statue. Her face was very dark. I realized I had made a mistake because it was her day and we didn't pray the rosary.

So I pointed to the Virgin's face and asked Larry to verify what I saw. He agreed it had turned pinkish. Then he said, "Probably the Blessed Mother wants you to write your story." I didn't answer Larry because I had to figure out what the Blessed Mother really wanted me to do. That night I dreamt about Father Jim. He was sitting on our porch autographing books that lots of people brought him. Sometimes I can tell right away the meaning of my dreams. But I had a hard time deciphering this dream.

I decided to go to St. Joseph Church in Lancaster, where the Monstrance holding the consecrated Host is displayed for adoration 24 hours a day. I implored Jesus to enlighten me. After genuflecting in front of the consecrated Host, I got a book to read from the pocket of the pew. Monsignor Felix Losito, the pastor of Holy Rosary Church in Reading, Pennsylvania, wrote the book. His photo was inside the cover. He had heard my confession once, when we visited his church. I didn't see his face in the darkened confessional box, but I was struck by his voice and was convinced he was a holy man. Here I was actually reading his book and realizing my faith journey was not unique.

The monsignor had the same experiences I had, except he did not mention dreaming about Jesus and the Blessed Virgin as I did. I was thinking he is more worthy than I to dream about Jesus and His mother, because I had committed grievous sins in the past. While meditating on the book in front of the Blessed Sacrament, I had a vision of the Blessed Mother. She was beautiful, with straight blonde hair, and looked to be in her 20s. And she was dressed all in white. It flashed in my mind that she wanted me to write my story with the help of Father Jim. She told me my story is compelling, and that whoever will read my book will know God is merciful and there is hope of redemption.

That was when my dream of Father Jim autographing the books made sense to me. However, as I said in the introduction of this book, I was afraid to write my story. Besides fearing being ridiculed and being called delusional, I had committed sins in my young adulthood I wasn't proud of and could not possibly mention in a book. I got the 10 pages I wrote for Maryann and read it once more. I thought if I added a bit to it, the Blessed Virgin would be satisfied.

Shortly thereafter, as I wrote in this book's introduction, I had the painful incident in my school that brought me to my doctor. An ultrasound and other tests showed I had ovarian cancer. To verify the doctor's first findings, I also had an MRI. While waiting for the results of the MRI, I continued to suffer terrible pains and was terrified. I lost my appetite. I was thinking the Blessed Mother really wanted me to write my full story. So I bargained with her. I said, "If you will ask your Son to heal me, I will write my full story."

Two weeks later I went back to my family doctor for the results. He said, "You are cancer-free." What he and a colleague had seen before was gone. He said it was a miracle brought about by prayer. He knew that Larry and my friends were all praying for a miracle of healing for me.

On September 30, 2007, we went to see the Filipina nuns at Cabrini Academy in Reading to buy the book by Monsignor Losito because I wasn't able to finish it at St. Joseph Church. Sister Marie said the monsignor was actually at the school attending a fund-raiser in the social hall. Larry, Maryann, and I could go to see him. When I saw the monsignor, I told him I had wanted to meet him ever since I heard his voice while confessing to him. I told him I knew him to be a holy man and I was very interested to buy his book. To my surprise, the monsignor said he would give it to me for free and to please pray for him. He gave me not one but five books, all autographed by him, plus one CD of church hymns.

On our way home, Larry, Maryann, and I dropped by St. Joseph Church for adoration. We lit a candle and prayed the luminous mysteries of the rosary for Monsignor Losito's intentions and for the success of his book.

Since reading the monsignor's book, I've given copies as gifts to people on Christmas and Easter. Whenever I have a chance in schools where I substitute teach and in conferences or classes I attend, I give them away as part of my evangelization. I also give the book to Protestants who were previously Catholic. Some of them have been difficult to deal with because they will tell you they aren't interested.

However, only one person actually rejected the book. I worked with this person in one classroom for five months, and she was the most difficult person I worked with in my six years as a substitute teacher. Before the school year ended, I encountered a verse in Matthew 6:19. It says you can prove to yourself that God is your most important treasure when you do not store up worldly treasures. Instead you should store up treasures in heaven. When I read this, I had an idea. I gave the book to this lady together with my diamond gold bracelet. It worked. She accepted both. After I gave her the book and my piece of jewelry, I noticed a change in her behavior. She wasn't irritably yelling at the kids anymore and she stopped gossiping. So I am sure she read Monsignor Losito's book. ☫

24
Accounts Taken from My 2007 Journal

January 15, 2007

I didn't sign up to go to the March for Life in Washington, D.C. However, the night before the bus departed, I dreamt I was with the same group of people who went in previous years. When I woke up at 5 a.m., I contacted my friend in charge of the bus and asked her if there was a seat available for me. She said there actually was one seat and it was paid for. The person who paid for it changed her mind, so I took the spot and just gave a donation. Since then, Larry and I have attended the March for Life every year in January.

November 26, 2007

Finally I received an e-mail from Father Jim agreeing to help me write and edit my story.

December 8, 2007

On the day of the feast of the Immaculate Conception, we went to Mass as a family at OMPH. I served as Eucharistic minister. I was abstaining from eating meat this Advent season, but I made an exception on the feast of the Immaculate Conception. As our pastor mentioned in his homily, the feast of the Immaculate Conception is a diamond of the Catholic Church because the Blessed Mother said yes to God that she would bear the Son of God, our Savior. We went to a restaurant to celebrate.

Then I called Father Jim and talked over some parts of my life to include in my book. I mentioned things I did that I kept from him when we were in Egypt, like my rigid fasting and abstaining from meat during Lent.

December 12, 2007

I attended Mass since it was the feast of Our Lady of Guadalupe of Mexico. Our Lady of Guadalupe played a very important role in my life and through her intercession my prayers were granted. Carolann, a very close friend for almost eight years, accidentally bumped a car at St. Joseph Church. Maryann and I were entering the parking lot to attend adoration when we saw her dent the car as she was driving out of the parking lot. I changed my mind and we went a couple of miles east to St. Anthony of Padua Church, where a cloak of Our Lady of Guadalupe is displayed. Maryann and I prayed to the Lady to help Carolann. When we got home I called her. She told me the police came and were very kind. They told her she could go home. If there would be no complaint from the owner of the car, then it was okay with them. I thought it was unusual that Carolann didn't get a ticket and I attributed that to Our Lady of Guadalupe's intercession.

I'd been looking for a statue of Our Lady of Guadalupe for some time. After this incident, while shopping at Walmart, Maryann saw a 5-foot statue of Our Lady of Guadalupe. She wanted me to buy it right away but I hesitated because it wasn't in a box. I asked for a box from the department clerk. She told me somewhat crossly that this one statue must have been mistakenly delivered to the store because they don't carry religious objects to sell.

I bought it anyway because I was sure it was meant for me. From Walmart we went straight to OMPH to ask Father Pat to bless the statue. The secretary said the pastor had left and would return in an hour. However, Father Pat arrived just as we were leaving. I told him how I bought the statue. He seemed very happy to bless it because he has a strong devotion to the Blessed Mother. He then carried Our Lady of Guadalupe to our car, making sure the unboxed statue was positioned well amid Maryann's messy stuff in the back seat.

My statue of our Lady of Guadalupe is now displayed in our living room. It stands beside my Fatima statue and the statues of St. Pio and the holy infant of Jesus that I brought from Italy and that was blessed by Pope Benedict XVI. In October 2011, we asked Father Pat to bless Maryann's bedroom. As soon as he entered our front doorway, he noticed the Fatima statue. He said to me, "Look at your statue, Linda. She's smiling and her cheeks have turned pinkish." I thought I was the only one who sees changes in my Fatima statue. But my statue showed a miracle to Father Pat because he is very devoted to the Blessed Mother. ✞

25
Weekend Marriage Encounter

We thought our relationship as a married couple was fine until I saw the couple who was going to conduct a Marriage Encounter seminar in our church on the weekend of February 27 to March 1, 2009. I saw something in their relationship that was missing in ours. They seemed not to be ashamed to show their love for each other in public. They held hands and there was a sparkle in their eyes. I was able to convince Larry that it would do us good to go, and we got a babysitter for the weekend we would be away.

We listened to four couples tell us how they improved their relationship by communicating with each other, understanding each other, and giving each other space to be their own person. One of the couples prayed for us during the weekend. We also had a priest tell us how he needed to learn to commit fully to his vocation, as well as how to deal with his fellow priests and the people he served. We were an interdenominational bunch, but the Catholics were able to attend Mass each day before the talks began.

I was correct in suspecting there was something missing in our relationship. I realized I was not totally open with Larry, nor did I trust him fully. Since taking the seminar, I've learned how to dialogue with Larry. We continue trying to improve our relationship as husband and wife because it is a covenant we made before God. By doing so, we are showing the goodness of God toward us and to people around us. ✝

26
How We Got Our Van

Sometime in late March 2009, I dreamt that we were trying to purchase a beige van. We drove onto a big yard. The dealer's office was painted beige too. When I awoke, I told Larry we were going to buy a van.

Larry replied, "I don't think so. Our car is still good."

Before this conversation, we had agreed to buy another car in three years. So I told Larry that I dreamt about it and woke up very early in the morning.

I said, "Larry, you know that whenever that happens, my dream will come true."

Anyhow, I told him, we needed to buy a van, not another car, because that's what I dreamt of.

Larry then said, "OK, but not this year."

Two days after my dream, we met Father Santan Pinto, a priest from India who was a close friend of Mother Teresa of Calcutta. He was at OMPH on a mission. Afterward, we invited him and his hosts to an Indian restaurant in Lancaster. We stopped by his hosts' house at 12:30 p.m. and told them to follow us in their car because we could not all fit in our small car. I thought to myself that if we had a van, we could all have gone in one vehicle.

The following day was Sunday and Larry had to bring Maryann to church to practice as part of the children's choir. A mile from church our car stopped. Maryann had to run to church to make it to her practice while Larry called AAA to drive him to the car repair shop. The amount they quoted to repair the car was huge, so Larry called me saying, "Well, we may have to buy a van sooner than we thought."

The next day in school, my co-worker recommended the dealer where she got her van at a reasonable price. Three days later, during the feast of the Annunciation, Larry went to the dealer after bringing me to work. As he was entering the lot, somebody was delivering a light-blue van. Larry was drawn to it because of the color—Mary's color—and it was her feast day. It took him only four hours from the time he decided to buy it until he signed the papers.

Larry picked me up from work and we went to the dealer to get our van. We then went to Father Pinto to deliver the Filipino food I'd cooked for him. We asked if he could bless the new van we bought. He said he would after he was done with his last day of mission at OMPH Church. Father Pinto gave his last talk; then he heard confessions. It was 11:30 p.m. before the last confession was heard. Afterward he and Larry went outside to our van. The priest blessed it outside and inside. It was almost midnight when Larry returned home. ✞

Linda and Larry passing the Statue of Liberty, July 4, 1996

Rainbow over Windber, Pennsylvania

Larry and Linda, five months pregnant,
at Bethesda Naval Hospital

Our first home blessing at Londonderry Apartments,
Gaithersburg, Maryland, September 15 ,1996; from left:
Josie, Fr. Filardi, Larry and Linda Lint, and Dennis Galvin

Roy Lint holding 12-day-old
Maryann Lint for baptism,
August 10, 1997

Maryann and Linda, October 23, 1997

Family in Maconacon; from left: Papang, Linda, Larry,
Jerilyn, Mamang, and Maryann (front left), February 2000

Linda flanked by Jerilyn and Jerry with Maryann in front,
surrounded by Maconacon students, February 2000

Linda receives her Certificate of
Citizenship, October 13, 2000, at
Johnstown, Pennsylvania

Fr. Jim celebrating Mass at our Ephrata
home, December 2003

With Fr. James Small (who blessed our
Ephrata home in 2001, and us on our
10th wedding anniversary, February 1, 2006)
in the sacristy of OMPH Church, Ephrata

The body of St. John Neumann
at his shrine in Philadelphia

Grotto of the Blessed Virgin Mary behind Our Mother
of Perpetual Help Church, Ephrata

Sr. Doris (front left) with companions and Maryann,
Bernardine convent, Stamford, Connecticut

Fr. Jim and National Pilgrim Virgin statue
of Our Lady of Fatima at Lint home in
Ephrata, 2004

From left: Henrietta Mondo, Mary Crawford, Fr. Pinto,
Linda Lint, and Sr. Marietta at home of Christine Hummer,
Birdsboro, Pennsylvania, July 3, 2010

Maryann and Bishop Kevin Rhoades at Harrisburg Diocese retreat at Basilica of the Immaculate Conception, Washington, D.C., October 24, 2009

Maryann on her confirmation day, with Bishop Joseph J. McFadden and her sponsor and aunt, Audree Lint, one of Larry's sisters, February 23, 2011

PART FOUR

27
I Dream of Italy

I dreamt I was riding an airplane to visit beautiful places with beautiful flowers. Some of the houses were the color of terra cotta. I saw myself walking on narrow cobblestoned streets with beautiful views everywhere and some water fountains.

When I woke up I told Larry we might be going somewhere and we are going to ride in an airplane. He responded, "Yes, I am thinking to go to Alabama to visit the site of EWTN and also Mother Angelica this coming summer. But we are not riding in an airplane. We are going by car."

I strongly told him I knew I was going to this place in my dreams that I'd never seen before. He said he didn't think so because riding an airplane involved a lot of money, and we didn't have enough money to spend this time because we'd just bought our van.

On April 1, we drove to the St. Pio Centre to join the prayer group. After prayers, someone announced that the body of St. Pio had been exhumed and would be displayed to the public until September, when his body would be returned to his tomb. He mentioned that anyone interested in joining the pilgrimage slated for the end of April needed to hurry since there were just three seats left on the plane.

I told Larry I really wanted to go on this pilgrimage. Larry reminded me again that we didn't have the money to pay for the plane ticket in advance.

So I said, "No problem, I will use my credit card. And if ever I need more money, I will borrow from my friends and tell them I will pay them back as soon as school starts and I will be working again. All through God's assistance, of course."

When Larry knew I was determined, he said, "OK. I don't want you to borrow from somebody else. We can take money from our savings, but you need to put it back."

Our original flight plan was the end of April, but that didn't push through because we lacked one person to complete the quota. Two hours after the group canceled the tour, somebody called to join. So the group scheduled another flight to leave on June 9. At first I was very disappointed when the first flight was canceled. Later, we all thanked God we didn't go at the end of April because, we found out, a strong earthquake hit Italy the day after we were due to arrive. Renovations were still going on when we landed there in June. ✞

28
Pilgrimage to Italy

The day of my flight I was more worried about my family than about myself. I was leaving Larry and Maryann to fend for themselves. As for me, I knew I was being taken care of by God through the Blessed Mother and St. Pio. And if something happened to me, I was in a state of grace because I was on an extraordinary pilgrimage. I was with a group of people of faith, we had Father Vince with us, and he would say Mass every day.

The first place we visited was the Church of Our Lady of the Rosary in Pompeii. St. Pio used to visit the statue of Our Lady of the Rosary when he was still alive. It was said that the last time he visited the church, he offered the Virgin a couple of long-stemmed roses that a family had given him in gratitude for answered prayer. To this day the roses remain fresh and the stems are still green.

Pompeii was destroyed by a volcanic eruption in A.D. 79. Christians settled the area in the third century and built the first church on the site. The third church, started by Bartolo Longo in 1876, is the current church of Our Lady of the Rosary (also known as Our Lady of Pompeii). The body of Longo, who spent most of his money making rosaries and publishing pamphlets on how to say the rosary, lies under the altar of the small chapel inside the church. His body is also incorrupt, like St. Pio's. The priest said Mass on the altar under which Longo's body lies. After the Mass I asked for Longo's intercession because I was partly doing what he had done, that is, giving people religious materials like rosaries and books because I wanted to help save souls.

✝

On June 11, 2009, we visited the house where St. Pio was born as well as the church where he was baptized. I was grateful for the chance to serve as one of the Eucharistic ministers when Father Vince said Mass. I offered my prayer intention for the Filipino nuns who were in charge of maintaining the church. Then I bought a 1.5-foot statue of St. Pio. (I carried this statue everywhere I went throughout the pilgrimage because I was afraid it might break inside my suitcase.)

After four hours there, we proceeded to San Giovanni Rotondo, where they put on view the incorrupt body of St. Pio. Built in honor of St. Pio, the hotel on the *rotondo* displays a big bronze statue of the saint near the entrance. Then we took a cab to the monastery because Father Vince was with us and he had difficulty walking up the hill. I took pictures of the monastery while waiting for our tourist guide to arrive. Meanwhile, the rest of my group had lined up in front of a monk outside the monastery to ask for his blessing.

Somebody in the group told me, "Linda, line up so the priest will bless you. But you need to give a donation."

I got in the line but realized I had no cash with me because I was using my credit card to buy things. When my turn came, I asked the monk if he could bless me even if I didn't have any money to donate. I told him I'm a Filipino and can speak Spanish. In Spanish, I told him I live in Pennsylvania and was in Italy to see St. Pio's body. Then I stepped out of the line. He pulled me back, smiled at me, scooped holy water with his hands from the small bowl, and poured it over my head. While the rest of the group got sprinkles of holy water, I was dripping with it. But I was grateful for the monk's special attention.

Inside the church, we watched a video of St. Pio's body being exhumed after 60 years. In the video, everybody wept tears of joy when they saw the saint's incorrupt body and smelled flowers. We were allowed to touch a relic of St. Pio before we were led to the basement of the church, where St. Pio's glass-encased body was displayed. I knelt three feet away from his body and prayed a whole rosary.

I offered my rosary for the intention of the people who handed me their prayer requests. I also offered it for my healing. Since 2005 I'd suffered stomach pains on and off. In 2007 I was diagnosed with ovarian cancer, but later an MRI showed I was cancer-free. However, I was having stomach pains once more. The pains had intensified the last three months before I took the pilgrimage.

On June 13 we went to the Church of St. Legontian in Lanciano, the site of the first Eucharistic Miracle. This wondrous event took place in the eighth century as a divine response to a Basilian monk who doubted the real presence of Jesus in the Eucharist. It is said that during the consecration, the host was changed into live Flesh and the wine was changed into live Blood. In 1970, at the initiative of Archbishop Pacifico Perantoni of Lanciano and with authorization from Rome, the relics were examined scientifically. Dr. Odoardo Linoli, professor of pathologic histology, conducted tests on the material and determined that the Flesh and the Blood were human and had the same blood type: AB.

At St. Legontian Church, I led the joyful mysteries of the rosary in honor of St. Anthony of Padua, since it was his feast day. Close to where the Eucharistic Miracle is kept under glass stands a big statue of St. Anthony with the Infant Jesus. I took a picture of the statue as well as the Eucharistic Miracle. Then I prayed for the priests and the lay ministers at OMPH Church, as well as for my healing. It was a very special day for me because I was seeing the Eucharistic Miracle behind Father Vince as he said Mass. Father Vince said he had the same feeling of privilege saying Mass where the miracle took place.

While I was meditating and praying in front of the Eucharistic Miracle, I thought how fortunate we are if, during Communion, we are offered the host as well as the wine—the complete Body and Blood of Jesus. Some just receive the host but ignore the wine. I think it is very important to receive both species if both are offered.

At 2 p.m. on June 13, we arrived at the Church of Loreto. I was with the group for a while. Then I decided to be alone so that I could manage my own time to look around and pray. I went to confession and then visited the shrine where the house of the Blessed Mother from Nazareth is displayed. This is the house where the Annunciation took place. The claim is that in the 17th century, when war was going on in Israel, an angel carried Mary's house from Nazareth to Loreto. Skeptics examined the stone and bricks of Mary's house. It does not match any stone and brick native to Italy. Our Lady of Loreto is the patron saint of the Italian Air Force.

On June 14, we arrived in Assisi at 10:30 a.m. We divided into two groups. One group would see the Church of the Holy Angels; the other, St. Francis' mansion. I joined the group interested in St. Francis. Our tour guide said St. Francis was a successful lawyer. His parents had a fine silk business and lived in a huge mansion. The young Francis loved parties and women. Then Jesus appeared to him several times and told him, "Follow me and repair my church."

St. Francis sold his horse and some of his family's silk and offered the gold to the priest, telling him to build a church with it. The priest, suspecting that something was amiss, went to St. Francis' father. St. Francis suffered the wrath of his Jewish father, who thought he was crazy. He locked St. Francis up in a closet in their mansion. His mother, a devout Catholic, released him. St. Francis so loved the Crucified Christ that he was given the stigmata. Thereafter he left his parents' home and begged for bricks to build the church.

Today St. Francis' church is huge and surrounded by additional walls. His bones are kept close to the ceiling. His clothing and gloves stained with blood from his stigmata are kept in the basement. The church also keeps the incorrupt body of St. Clare, to whom I prayed a specific prayer for Maryann. I asked St. Clare to guide her and I hoped that Maryann would serve God as St. Clare did. Then I offered a Mass for my intention and prayed that St. Francis and St. Clare would intercede on behalf of the people for whom I prayed.

I learned that St. Francis often had terrible stomach pains, and that eventually what caused those pains killed him. I was surprised to learn this because I too had been suffering from stomach pains. They got worse the closer I came to my departure for Italy. The pain, which lasted three to four hours, was like a sharp knife cutting across my belly. When it attacked me at work, I just bore it. I didn't want anything to happen that would stop me from going to Italy. I did go to my family doctor. He wanted to check me by performing a colonoscopy. But I had it scheduled for after my return from Italy, believing I would get healed while on the pilgrimage. Sure enough, I did not feel any pain while in Italy.

✝

We arrived at the Cathedral of Orvieto on June 15 to see a relic of the second Eucharistic Miracle. It is a white altar cloth with bloodstains. The second miracle happened when a priest saying Mass didn't believe in the true presence of Jesus in the host. For him, the Consecration was merely symbolic. So, when he broke the host, it bled and stained the altar cloth. An Italian scientist tested the blood. It is AB, the same blood type found in the first Eucharistic Miracle at Lanciano and on the Shroud of Turin.

On June 16, we visited the Basilica of St. Peter at the Vatican. I took some pictures inside the basilica as well as inside the museum and the Sistine Chapel. Afterward my roommate, Ana, and I went to St. Joseph Church, where the cloak of St. Joseph is preserved. There I offered a Mass for Larry. We then visited the Basilica of Mary Maggiore, where a relic from the wooden crib of the Baby Jesus and a piece of cloth of the Blessed Mother are displayed.

On June 17, we arrived at the Vatican at 8:30 a.m. for our papal audience. It was sunny and very hot, and we waited close to five hours before Pope Benedict XVI arrived. I did not see his face up close when he passed by to wave to us. After the pope talked and blessed us, my group left for lunch. I chose to skip lunch and stay behind. A lady was kind enough to make room for me so I could join a group of newly married couples who were to receive special blessings from the pope. I was only 10 feet away from him when he gave his blessings. I was amazed to see how young he looked compared to his photos. I missed my lunch as well as the group, but I was happy to see the pope up close.

In the afternoon, before rejoining my group, I visited the Basilica of St. Paul. I felt a good connection upon entering the church because I had graduated from St. Paul University in the Philippines and here I was in the place where his bones are kept.

Later, five of us made a side trip to Santa Croce Basilica before joining the rest of the group at the Basilica of St. John Lateran, where Father Vince was going to say Mass at 5 p.m. Santa Croce Basilica was not part of our itinerary, but Larry called from the States to tell me to find time to visit the church and see relics of the cross to which Jesus was nailed.

So, the day before, I asked my Italian roommate to make arrangements with our male tour guide to bring a few of us to Santa Croce before we went to St. John Lateran. However, the tour guide changed his mind because we would be hard pressed for time. I pointed out that the Santa Croce church wasn't far from St. John Lateran and I promised we would spend no more than 25 minutes there. We just needed to see the two true thorns, the nails, and the piece of wood with INRI (King of the Jews) written on it.

I could not seem to persuade him, so I decided to pray the rosary and ask Jesus to help us see his relic. While praying, I felt enveloped by a light, cold air even though it was in the middle of summer. I knew then that the Holy Spirit was beside me. When I was on my third decade of the joyful mysteries, the other tour guide, a woman, said she would bring us to Santa Croce if we promised to spend only 20 minutes there.

The four others with me told me they saw me praying and knew God would answer my prayers. It made me happy to know they recognized that nothing was impossible if God acted on it. Anyhow, we ended up staying more than 30 minutes at Santa Croce. My companions, who had been to Rome two or three times before, realized this was a very significant church. They wondered why it had never been part of their itinerary.

✝

During breakfast on our last day in Rome, Kerry, who worked at the St. Pio shrine in Barto, told us he dreamt that St. Pio said not to worry because he would be riding the same plane back to the States with us. What Kerry dreamt was true because my statue of St. Pio was going with me as part of my hand-carried luggage. At customs, the man asked what I was carrying. I uncovered the statue and said, "St. Pio." The man said, "Go on. It is Padre Pio."

On our flight from Rome to Frankfurt, Germany, the middle seat beside me was vacant, so I put the statue of St. Pio there. From Germany to Newark, New Jersey, the same thing happened. When we landed in Newark, I told the group that Kerry's dream was true: St. Pio was with us throughout our flight. He had his own seat beside me not once but twice. The group recognized it could not have been a coincidence that on both flights the seat beside me was vacant. It was St. Pio showing us a miracle. ✞

Linda with pilgrim companion Sophie
on road above Sorrento

Sanctuary in the Shrine
of Our Lady of the
Rosary, Pompeii

Padre Pio's exhumed body, displayed at the Shrine
of Padre Pio in San Giovanni Rotondo, Italy

Lanciano reliquary containing host and wine
transformed into Flesh and Blood; the Flesh
is in the upper reliquary and the Blood is
coagulated in the vial between the angels

Linda and fellow pilgrim at fountain in front of the Basilica di Santa Casa Loreto

Upper Church Sanctuary in the Basilica of St. Francis at Assisi

Room where St. Francis was imprisoned
by his father in Assisi

Linda with Franciscan monks at Assisi

Relics of the crucifixion collected by St. Helen, on display
in the Basilica of Santa Croce in Gerusalemme, Rome;
left: a piece of the good thief's cross;
top, from left: index finger of St. Thomas,
pieces of the scourging pillar, and
two thorns from the crown of Christ;
center: four pieces of Christ's cross in cruciform reliquary

Relic of the crucifixion collected by St. Helen: a piece
of the title that Pilate ordered hung on the upright
beam of Christ's Cross; on display in the
Basilica of Santa Croce in Gerusalemme, Rome

Relic of Christ's crib,
Basilica of Santa Maria
Maggiore, Rome

Blood-stained corporal at
Ovierto Church

Basilica of St. Paul

View of Santa Maria Maggiore from Piazza dell'Esquilino

Statue of St. Joseph and the Holy Child in the garden of the Basilica di San Giuseppe al Trionfale, Rome, home to the Pious Union of St. Joseph

PREFETTURA DELLA CASA PONTIFICIA

Udienza Generale di Sua Santità
Benedetto XVI

mercoledì 17 giugno 2009 - ore 10,30

14013

Il biglietto è del tutto gratuito – Ce billet est gratuit – This ticket is entirely free
Die Eintrittskarte ist kostenlos – La entrada es gratis – O bilhete é gratuito

Ticket for papal audience, June 17, 2009

Papal audience, St. Peter's Square, June 17, 2009

Air passenger Padre Pio; this statue traveled home from
Rome with Linda, in the only empty seats on two flights

PART FIVE

29
Answered Prayer

I scheduled a colonoscopy before going to Italy; so as soon as we returned, I went for the surgery. My surgeon had also just come from Italy. He said, "Let us pray it is not cancerous."

He removed a big polyp and a bunch of little ones from my colon that he thought were the cause of my terrible pain the past few months. However, the pain had not recurred when I was in Italy. I'd prayed for healing at the different religious sites, and I knew for sure that God would grant my prayers through the intercession of the Blessed Mother, St. Francis, and St. Pio.

After the operation I needed to wait two weeks for the results. I was scared, imagining how we would cope if I had cancer. But I trusted God, who knows what's best for me. After a week my main doctor left a message on our telephone telling me the polyps he removed were benign.

We visited Father Jim in Washington, D.C., a couple of times before he was finally transferred to Myanmar from Bangkok in October 2009. I felt sad that he was going away to where it would be hard to reach him. He had been my spiritual director for more than 15 years. ✝

30
Miracle of the Sun

On October 10, 2009, I went to Mass in the morning and returned to OMPH in the evening for the novena to Our Mother of Perpetual Help. Father Pat talked about the story of the three children the Blessed Virgin appeared to at Fatima, Portugal, in the early 20th century. He said they were so scared when the policemen questioned them about what they saw—that is, the Blessed Mother and a dancing sun. As I listened to Father Pat, I got scared too, imagining what people might think of me if I told them I also saw a sun similar to what the three kids saw.

That's why I joined the rosary rally at OMPH Church instead of going to the Blue Army Shrine of the World Apostolate of Our Lady of Fatima in New Jersey, where the Miracle of the Sun is recalled each year. I'd heard that a few other people there had witnessed a dancing sun, and I was able to talk to one of them. Her experience bore strong similarities to mine, but I was reluctant to talk about my own experience.

After the novena I decided not to go to confession because I was afraid I might mention the sun to the priest. Will he believe me or will he ridicule me if I tell him that on September 27, 2007, at 8:05 a.m. I saw a big orange sun bouncing in the sky while I was driving home? It frightened me, so when I reached home I ran inside the house. In a split second I ran out, realizing this must be a miracle. I saw the sun again on top of the big tree in our backyard. This time it was like a big crystal globe spinning red, white, and blue.

When I came back from OMPH Church I told Larry I might not continue writing my story because I was scared.

While I was telling him, the chain my Miraculous Medal was on broke. Larry said, "Now your Miraculous Medal broke because you keep on resisting."

The following day, on my way back home after driving Maryann to school, I had the urge to turn left instead of right. I passed by a tree and spotted a cross covered with nails. The cross was blinking like stars at night when the sky is clear. I had passed that road and the tree a couple of times before but I had never seen the cross.

It dawned on me that this was the sign I was asking for. Every now and then I would doubt my dreams and visions as figments of my imagination, then ask for a sign. I even asked a close friend at OMPH whom I consider to be a holy woman if she ever dreamt of the Blessed Mother and Jesus. She told me she never did but wished she had. To this day I still question myself: Why me? I'm not worthy!

When I returned home after seeing the blinking cross, I went to our little chapel to pray the rosary. In front of the statues Larry and I had collected from Jerusalem, Egypt, Italy, and the Philippines, I asked for forgiveness from God and the Blessed Mother. I promised to continue writing my story if that was what she wanted from me. After I was done praying, the story of Saul came to my mind. On the road to Damascus, he heard God calling, "Saul! Saul! Why are you persecuting me?" Like Saul, I was persecuting God because of my skepticism. ✝

31

My Mother Passes Away

I went home again 10 years after Larry, Maryann, and I visited the Philippines. This time it wasn't a happy visit. Mamang died unexpectedly on February 28, 2010.

Jerilyn and her brand-new husband, Bert, met me at the airport. They drove me to my brother Herbert's home in Tuguegarao, where Mamang's body lay in state.

"What was the cause of her death?" I asked tearfully.

"She fell . . . and died," Papang told me.

The real cause of her death was hidden from me until I was able to communicate with my mother while I was praying a rosary for the repose of her soul. The first thing she asked me to do was to go to Our Lady of Piat and pray for her soul. Then she said I needed to ask Auring, one of my sisters-in-law, to help me find out why she died. Auring didn't really know, so on the day of the burial she looked for a clue. When Mamang's coffin was opened for the last time at the cemetery, I was too distraught with grief to notice anything. But Auring saw a black mark on my mother's left eye. She went to me and urged me to question the embalmer.

Immediately after the burial I asked the embalmer to tell me all he knew about the cause of my mother's death. That was when he said my niece Catherine, whom I paid to take care of Mamang, told him she wanted to keep it a secret from me. However, the embalmer put the real cause of Mamang's death in his report. It was internal hemorrhage, probably due to the fall. According to him there was a large amount of clotted blood in her brain when he did the embalmment.

I'd never been as angry as I was after hearing that. I blamed myself for getting someone who could not be trusted to take care of my mother. I was so sad knowing that Papang also knew how Mamang died but kept it a secret from me too.

I was supposed to visit my mother in June during Maryann's school break so that she could accompany me. But it did not happen because Mamang died earlier. It was too hard for me to accept. I cried so hard that I felt a pain in my chest, like a sword had struck me from front to back, and I could not breathe.

The day after Mamang's burial, I went to the shrine of Our Lady of Piat. The temperature was about 97 degrees Fahrenheit. According to my relatives, it had not rained in Cagayan Valley for almost six months. Indeed, I noticed how dry and brown the countryside was. At the shrine I first prayed for my mother's soul, as she wanted me to do. Then I begged the Lady to intercede on behalf of the farmers and make it rain.

Twenty minutes after I left the shrine, there was a strong downpour. It rained close to one hour and everyone around was overjoyed. I recognized that once again the Blessed Mother granted my prayers. When I called Larry to share the news of the miracle, he was in the home of a parishioner who was hosting the Pilgrim Virgin Statue of Our Lady of Fatima. They were just about to pray the rosary. But first, he told them about the miracle.

I stayed three weeks with Jerilyn and got to know her better. What I saw did not please me. She acted like a spoiled brat and did not treat her husband well. "You have to change your ways or your marriage won't be successful," I told her.

I found out she had not gone to church for a long time. "You need to go back to God and to pray," I advised her.

She and her husband were both employed but were not making enough to make ends meet. "You were in third-year nursing. You should have finished your studies and gotten a better job instead of getting married," I scolded her.

Of course Jerilyn was not happy with my fault-finding. I had not been there for her when she was growing up, so why should I discipline her now, she told me bitterly. She also told me that if she disappointed me, I also disappointed her. It was hard for her to continue nursing, she complained, because I didn't send enough money for her and her brother's studies.

This was a surprise to me. Twice a year I sent one of my sisters-in-law more than enough money to cover their studies. It turned out that this sister-in-law gave my children only half of the money and used the rest herself. She also discouraged Jerilyn from continuing her studies, saying that nursing jobs in the Philippines were scarce and paid so little.

"And she said I could not go to the States because you were not going to get me. That's why I decided to get married," Jerilyn said.

She forgave me after I told her the truth. I also said that although I wasn't physically present as a mother, I always thought about them, always prayed for them, and always sent them money.

After that, we went to a restaurant. There was an old lady inside begging for food. The staff was trying to chase her away. I told Jerilyn to bring the lady to our table and ask her to point to whatever food she liked and I would pay for it. This was to set an example of generosity for my daughter. Jerilyn was touched and now is generous to those around her.

In 2011, Jerilyn gave me my first grandchild. We talked over the phone and she told me she wanted to finish her studies. I promised her that if she graduated and passed the U.S. board exam for nurses, I would help her get to America. She also told me that she now prays and attends Sunday Mass.

I then went to visit my son, Jerry, but could stay only two days. That time was enough for Jerry and me to air our regrets and disappointments with each other. What bothered me most was that my son had a live-in girlfriend.

"You must either get married, Jerry Boy, or separate," I admonished. I told him I did not want him to go the way his father and I went. "I was able to leave your father and straighten my life. You can too," I said.

In reply he told me how sad he was when I went abroad and married Larry. "I felt Larry grabbed my happiness away," Jerry said.

That wounded me deeply but I desisted from pointing out to him what a violent, abusive man his father was. All I said was, "I am legally married now and this path I took has brought me closer to God."

What he said next surprised me. "OK, I give up." What did he mean by that? I soon understood when I visited my uncle and found Rolly standing across the street from my uncle's house. To avoid having to talk to him, I left through the back door. Apparently Jerry had told his father I was going to visit my uncle. My son was trying to get Rolly and me back together. ✞

32
Weddings and Reunions

Mamang had been praying a long time for my brother Victor and his wife, Auring, to be married in the Catholic Church. Larry and I had also been praying to Our Lady of Manaoag, a favorite icon in Pangasinan Province.

She died without seeing her prayers answered. So, on the day of Mamang's funeral, I awoke Victor and Auring at 3 a.m. I told them we needed to discuss a very important matter beside our mother's coffin because, although she was already dead, she was listening. I asked them to promise our mother that they were going to be married in the Catholic Church just as she wanted. I said I would pay for the church wedding. I wanted to do it for Mamang's sake as well as for the salvation of their souls. They said yes, and set the wedding for March 26.

The day before they were wed I dreamt that Mamang was smiling and telling me she would be at the church during the wedding. She told me I needed to provide for a celebration afterward. So I gave Auring money to cook *pansit* noodles.

On March 26, Our Lady of Manaoag also granted my request to see my brother Danny, whom I hadn't seen for 22 years, that is, since I left the Philippines. Danny wasn't able to attend our mother's funeral because he lived along the coast and the weather was very bad at that time. When the weather cleared, he decided not to come to my brother Herbert's home in Tuguegarao because Mamang was already buried. But I prayed to Our Lady of Manaoag to change Danny's plans. I wanted to see him before I left for the States.

On the day of Victor and Auring's wedding, Herbert called me with the news that Danny and his son had arrived in Tuguegarao. They had walked for five days because they could not ride a motorboat. The waves were too big. Then Danny was on the phone, crying. He said he wanted to see me before I went back to the States. He said he brought along the picture of Our Lady of Fatima that I'd sent him years ago from the States. He said he'd been praying to her since the day he received it. Then he said he too wanted to get married in the Catholic Church.

My meeting with Danny was very emotional. We hugged each other and cried. Danny hadn't believed in a God who cared for us who we could pray to. I remember that whenever he saw my father kneeling before statues of the Blessed Mother and the Santo Niño, he would tell my father that prayers were useless. Now here he was, praying daily to Our Lady of Fatima and wanting his marriage to be blessed by God.

I arranged for Danny to receive the sacrament of confirmation. This was a requirement in order to be married in the Catholic Church. Then I gave him money for his wedding expenses. He and his wife did get married in their parish after I returned to the States. ✝

33
Holy Week

My final week in the Philippines coincided with Holy Week. On Holy Wednesday I went to confess my sins. I also encouraged some of my relatives who had been away from the Church for several years to go to confession. Two of them were Jerilyn and my niece Catherine.

On Holy Thursday I took the bus to Manila, from where I would fly home to the States after Easter Sunday. Accompanying me was Catherine. My initial anger at her for indirectly causing my mother's death had turned to pity and compassion. During the nine-hour trip, I gave her lots of advice. I told her she needed to change her ways. I found out she was in a relationship with a married man. This was the reason she had neglected my mother. She was always going on dates with him. I told her it was good she made her confession but that wasn't enough. She also had to allow the Holy Spirit to enter her soul and take control of her life.

As we passed one of the towns of Pampanga Province, we saw a procession of penitents. They were carrying heavy wooden crosses and allowing themselves to be flagellated. They were on their way to San Fernando, the capital city of Pampanga, to participate in a live crucifixion at 3 p.m. on Good Friday.

The sight of the bloodied penitents brought back memories of the time in second-year high school when I saw a live crucifixion in Cagayan Valley. This man carried a heavy wooden cross around town from Holy Monday to Good Friday. On the day of the crucifixion, someone continuously flogged him until he was all bloodied. I was one of a huge crowd following him. Then, at 3 p.m., he placed his cross on the ground and lay down on it. They tied his arms to the crossbeam and drove a nail into each of his palms. They raised him up for a minute or two. Then they carefully laid him back on the ground, removed the nails, poured alcohol on his wounds and bandaged his palms. He talked to us afterward as though nothing had happened. He had been undergoing crucifixion for a few years as penance for his sins and to give witness that there truly is a God. According to him, after he bathes on Easter Sunday, his wounds become nearly imperceptible.

As I recalled the pains to which this man subjected himself as penance for his sins, I became more courageous to finish this book and to face the shame of exposing the secret sins of my past, all for God's glory.

We arrived in Manila late Thursday evening. On Good Friday, I went with three relatives to the Church of the Black Nazarene. It was packed with devotees inside and outside. We were just lucky we were able to touch the feet of the statue of the Black Nazarene before they cut off the line of people. For Filipinos, it is really a big deal to be able to go inside the super-packed church on Good Friday, much more so if one is able to touch the Black Nazarene. This church in downtown Manila was where I made my last confession, with tears flowing copiously down my face, before leaving the Philippines for Kuwait in 1989.

On Good Friday, my brother Victor and I attended Mass. I was happy to see that Filipinos still carried our tradition and culture since I left the Philippines in 1989. A majority of the ladies were wearing veils and they were dressed modestly. I didn't see any woman in jeans.

✠

I flew back home and arrived in Philadelphia on Wednesday after Easter Sunday at 4 p.m. I was so glad to see Larry and Maryann. That evening I was able to attend the Wednesday novena devotion in honor of Our Mother of

Perpetual Help at OMPH Church. I had never missed this devotion unless I was sick or out of the country. It was early spring and the day was sunny and balmy. And I knew that the Blessed Mother was with me. ☦

Jerry's graduation from STI
College, Tuguegarao, 2009

Jerilyn's wedding at Our Lady of the Pillar
Church in Cauayan, Isabela, Philippines

Our Lady of Manaoag

Jerilyn with her
daughter and Papang

The Black Nazarene

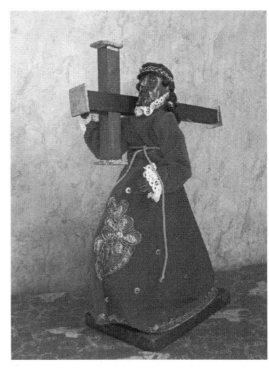

PART SIX

34
Song of Joseph

When I arrived home I received an e-mail from Father Jim, who was still in Bangkok, Thailand. He told me to rush my book to him to edit before he left for Myanmar (Burma) to teach English. He said the Internet connection there was iffy. I replied that I needed to include my trip to Italy and to the Philippines, and I still had to finish the manuscript. So I stopped sending him e-mails and just waited for him to get in touch with me. After April 2010, we had no communication. While I was slowly finishing my book, I prayed to the Blessed Mother to give me something to do that will proclaim the glory of God in another way.

Three days after I prayed, my friend Marichelle told me she was interested in bringing to Lancaster County an original musical about St. Joseph, the father of Jesus. She said *Song of Joseph* was commissioned by the Oblates of St. Joseph in the Philippines to proclaim the goodness of the man who loved and protected Jesus and the Blessed Mother. It was written and composed by Filipinos and had an all-Filipino cast. She had seen a DVD of it and was truly impressed with the music and lyrics as well as with the actors and the production values. She told me she thought it would do very well in Lancaster County, with its large religious community. However, she said she needed two other Filipinos to help her co-produce and co-sponsor it here. Marichelle also told me that the faith of Fides Cuyugan-Asensio, the writer, had become stronger while she researched the life of Joseph and that many of her lines were inspired by the Holy Spirit.

I immediately saw this musical as the Blessed Mother's answer to my prayer and said yes without first consulting Larry. But Larry, who is deeply devoted to St. Joseph, was all for it. Rene Oliveros, another Filipino, also said yes. So it was a go.

We had trials when we started this project. Our first venue fell through a few weeks before the performance date, October 9, 2010. Our second venue, the Lancaster Mennonite High School (LMHS) auditorium, was not available on October 9, but we were told to wait anyway just in case there was a cancellation.

Meanwhile, Marichelle started looking seriously at a more expensive but smaller venue. I told her to wait one more day while I prayed on it. I went to St. Joseph Church in Lancaster and prayed before the statue of St. Joseph. I told him the musical was all about him and that he needed to make a miracle so that we could get the LMHS auditorium. It had 800 seats, not counting the balcony, and it was within our budget. I promised to come back and light a candle once he got the LMHS auditorium for us.

As soon as I left the church, my telephone rang. It was Marichelle telling me that LMHS had called saying there was a cancellation and we could use the auditorium on October 9. Truly it was a miracle from St. Joseph!

Marichelle thought it would be good if we could get St. Joseph Church to lend its name as sponsor of the show. We went to see Monsignor Thomas Smith, pastor of the church, with an offer. We would give 200 tickets for the church to sell and they could keep the money to fund their parish programs. In exchange, the monsignor would write an endorsement and dedication that we would include in our playbill. Before we went to the monsignor, I went to the statue of St. Joseph and lit the candle I had promised him. Then we headed to talk to the monsignor, without any doubt in my heart that he would say yes.

The show was a success. There were features in several papers as well as posters in Lancaster County's Catholic and Christian churches. More than 400 people saw and enjoyed it. We as producers and sponsors opened our pocketbooks to produce the best show we could afford. We were not able to recover our expenses, but the money we spent was well worth it. Larry and I believed that this was not our money. It was God's and we gave it back to Him for His greater glory. ☫

35
To Write or Not to Write

The year 2011 was a blank year for me. I didn't have any special dreams, so I decided to join the Disciples of Jesus and Mary (DJM) order under the direction of Father Santan Pinto. To join the order, I needed to submit my plan of life for Father Pinto's approval. After his approval, I also needed to go through his book.

As I read about his life and experiences, I saw a resemblance with what I had already written for my book. So I told the leaders of DJM that I needed to stop reading and just commit to my plan of life. I also told them I was writing a book along the same lines as Father Pinto's and that my spiritual advisor, Father Jim, was reading it before he left for Myanmar. I did not tell them that the writing of my book was on hold because, again, I was plagued with doubts.

I was not yet fully accepted into the DJM order when Father Pinto died in a horrible accident when he went back to India. The last time I saw him was during a DJM gathering. I cooked *kare-kare*, a Filipino dish he liked very much, and served it to him. When it was time to go, I asked for a special blessing from him. He held my head for 20 minutes and gave me his blessing. This holy man was filled with the Holy Spirit and as he blessed me, I felt the Spirit as well.

✤

Larry was on a business trip and I was sleeping alone when I dreamt of a lady wearing a veil. She was standing outside our room and her face was in darkness. I noticed she had a nice figure and a light, sweet voice. "Hello," she said. "Hello," she said again. I immediately woke up and looked at the time. It was 3 a.m.

Who could she be? Before I went to bed, I had been mulling over a call I received from the common-law wife of my son, Jerry. She had advanced tuberculosis and needed money for an operation to save her life. I really didn't want to help her unless she either married or left my son. But perhaps the lady was the Blessed Mother telling me I needed to send money right away to help this young woman. So I did, and helped save her life.

I now know the Blessed Mother was telling me that if I had the resources to help people in need, I should do so without any preconditions. And I added this to my plan of life that I submitted to the DJM order.

I was positive that the lady in my dream was the Blessed Mother, but I wanted to know why her face was dark. I told a close friend at OMPH Church about the dream. She told me right away that the Lady in my dream might be Our Lady of Czestochowa. I said, "Oh, yes!" I am very devoted to Pope John Paul, so each time I visit the St. Pio shrine, I also pray to the pope. The icon of Our Lady of Czestochowa is behind the pope's statue and I also pray to her.

A week after the dream I went to St. John Neumann Church for 9 a.m. Mass followed by rosary in honor of Our Lady of Medjugorje. Afterward, a close friend gave me a book about Medjugorje written by Mary Hendel McCafferty. In one of the pages she described how she felt when she saw the miraculous sun. I was amazed because her description of the "bouncing" sun was almost the same as the sun I saw on my way home and on top of our tall tree at the back of our house. I knew then that I wasn't imagining things. What I saw was real. And that was my final push to finish my book for the purpose of evangelization. ✝

36
St. Pio's Miracles

On August 19, 2012, we attended a special event at the shrine of St. Pio in Barto. On display were close to a hundred relics of saints, some of them transported from Italy. Donations were asked for, with the promise that the donors' names would be posted. Larry and I requested that our names be posted under St. Pio, St. Joseph, or St. Francis, but the lady volunteer said we could not choose.

I asked Larry to approach Julia Calandra-Lineberg, the daughter of the founder of the National Centre for Padre Pio, while I prayed to the Holy Spirit to link our names with the right relic. Julia replied that the relics we had asked for were all taken. But, she suggested, how about the Blessed Virgin instead? When Larry came back to say that our names would be placed under the Virgin's relic, I was surprised and delighted. We did not ask for the Virgin's relic in the first place because we thought it would be taken first. I was so happy about it. I knew it was not a coincidence that the Blessed Mother reserved her relic for us.

One day in 2010, we were going somewhere in the car when Larry noticed slight bleeding from my left ear. He was startled and stopped the car. His first thought was to bring me to the nearest hospital. However, he thought again and asked me if I had been praying for somebody.

I said, "Yes, my sister-in-law Marivic. She asked me to pray for her because her left ear is swollen and she can't go to work."

Larry replied, "Oh." And we continued on our way. Larry knew from past incidents that I was just participating in the pain of the person I was praying for.

Later that day, Marivic called to thank me because the swelling in her ear was gone. I understand that the healing power of prayer comes from God but I am reluctant to say yes to everyone who asks me to pray for a healing. I need discernment. Is God's will in this, and am I willing to suffer as well?

My involvement with healing prayer began in the Philippines in 1988 when Tang Totoy, who has healing powers, gave me a special prayer he wanted me to read every day. He said he was giving it to me because he saw something in me. He then showed me how he performed his healing. First he lit a candle. If the flame was bright and strong, he took that as a positive sign from God. He then touched the person and prayed over him. One time, we went to the home of a mother whose baby was very ill. When he lit the candle, I could hardly see the flame. He sadly told the mother he could do nothing for the baby.

Like Tang Totoy, I need to discern whether I should pray for a certain person or not. I don't like to perform healing or pray over someone unless the person believes. If I determine that a person needs prayer, I will give the person a picture and a relic of St. Pio. Or if my feeling is intense, I tell the person to fast either on the first Wednesday of the month in honor of the Blessed Mother or on First Friday to honor Jesus. I pray as well. And if the person is healed, it all comes from God.

☦

The late Father John Dorf, who was one of the parish priests in OMPH Church, once told me that sometimes, while praying in front of a statue of the Virgin Mary, he would notice the statue smiling at him or blinking her eyes. He took this as a sign that God was pleased with him. I too

175

experience this phenomenon with my Fatima statue. As I mentioned earlier, I notice her cheeks turn pink and she smiles if she is pleased with me. I also have seen her face darken a few times when she isn't pleased.

A few years back, I wanted to transfer my Fatima statue from the living room to the all-purpose room across from it. Before doing so, I bought a can of paint to freshen the room. On my way home, the can turned upside down and the cover fell off, spilling blue paint on the floor of the passenger side. I had a hard time cleaning it up. Then I bought another can of paint.

The following day, while bringing Maryann home from school, I told her we were going straight home because I wanted to paint the all-purpose room. I heeded the stop sign at an intersection, noticed I had the right of way, and crossed it. Then I heard a loud noise and saw our car smoking. I was in shock and made attempts to continue driving.

But Maryann, who was in the back seat, said, "Mommy, we have to get out. The car is smoking and your face is bleeding."

Only then did I realize that we'd had an accident. Apparently we were hit while we were crossing the intersection. Maryann escaped without any bruises. She said she was protected by her guardian angel. The day before our accident, she had just learned about guardian angels.

They brought us to the hospital for a checkup. Luckily my injuries were not serious. I had neck pains for a while, but I didn't file any complaint against the driver because when I looked into her eyes just after the accident, she seemed very scared. So I pitied her instead.

When we reached home, I went to my Fatima statue and promised her I would keep her in the living room instead of trying to hide her. The first person who saw me after the accident was my friend Rita. She saw the bruises and wounds on my face and offered me Communion. Larry was on a business trip at that time, but my kind friends offered to bring Maryann to school daily because our car was totaled.

Anyhow, I applied St. Pio's oil to my face and asked him to heal the wounds so my face wouldn't look too bad for my rosary session, which was scheduled on St. Pio's birthday, exactly three days after the accident. Amazingly, thanks to St. Pio's intercession, the scab on my face was peeling off on his birthday.

✠

Andrea Ostrowski, a good friend who had four daughters, had been longing to have a son. I knew how desperately she and her husband wanted this, so I decided to touch her belly secretly. Then I lit a candle when we went to the St. Pio shrine in Barto, and I prayed for his intercession to favor my friend with a boy for her fifth pregnancy. She did get pregnant.

It happened that the day she delivered, I went for adoration at St. Joseph Church. On my way home, I stopped by a department store on a whim. Right near the entrance was a display of baby clothes on sale for fifty cents to a dollar. I thought of my friend who was due to deliver soon. I had a strong feeling she would have a boy, so I chose blue, green, and yellow outfits plus a red Santa Claus suit.

I called her as soon as I got out of the store and asked if she had already given birth. I said I had just bought some baby clothes for her. She said yes, she had given birth five hours earlier and it was a boy. I gave her the clothes and her baby was even able to wear the Santa suit for the christening because he was christened in December, before Christmas.

I am positive that Jesus, through the intercession of St. Pio, answered my prayer request since that was the only time I prayed specifically for a boy.

✠

A member of our parish was diagnosed with cancer and she was very scared of her upcoming surgery. I gave her the prayer card of St. Pio with his relic on it. I told her to pray to St. Pio on the day of her surgery. I also promised to pray and to light a candle at St. Pio's shrine before her operation. When she came back to church a week after her surgery, she announced that it had been successful. I whispered to her that I lit a candle for her at St. Pio's shrine. She said that during the operation she had felt cold air wrapped around her and had felt very peaceful.

There was also a boy in the parish who had cancer. His family was not close to us, but because I pitied the kid, I approached him one time and gave him the prayer card of St. Pio. I told the boy to pray to him and he said yes, he would. He also was healed.

I dreamt about one of the ladies from our church on the morning I was to go to 9 a.m. Mass. I approached her and asked how she was doing. She responded that she had cancer and was going for surgery. Just like the others, she was scared. I touched her gently and prayed secretly. I also lit a candle for her when we went to St. Pio's shrine. Again, the surgery was successful and she became cancer-free.

I met a lady at St. John Neumann Church. She was crying and desperate because she had no income and didn't know how the family would survive. Again, I gave her the prayer card of St. Pio. She was consoled because she said St. Pio was one of the patron saints of her deceased mother. After a week I went back to attend the church's rosary group. She approached me to tell me that St. Pio had answered her prayers. Her daughter had succeeded in an interview and gotten a job.

As she and I were talking about St. Pio, a Filipino approached us and asked about the saint. I told him the story of a friend from Windber who gained her eyesight after being legally blind for 38 years. I had prayed for her, and through the intercession of St. Pio she was healed and could drive without eyeglasses. He listened very intently. Then I gave him my last prayer card. Afterward he told me that he and his family had just moved to Lancaster from

New York. They had a son who was bipolar. No hospital wanted to accept him because he was very violent. On their own, they could not give him the care he needed to get well. He even refused to take his medications.

The following day I met his wife. She was desperate and crying. I told her I would pray for their son. I gave them St. Pio's oil to massage onto his head and told them to take St. Pio's card with his relic on it and read the prayer printed on the card. The next time I saw them they told me a hospital had finally accepted him. He was now willing to take his medication and was calmer as a result. I told them they needed to fast and abstain from eating meat especially on the first Wednesday and the first Friday of each month, and to offer their intention for the healing of their son.

It didn't take 15 days of praying and fasting for their son to be completely healed. I told them to offer a thanksgiving prayer at St. Pio's shrine, which they did. Two months later they opened a Filipino restaurant and store in Lancaster city. One time I visited their store and met their son. They wanted me to pray over him, but I decided just to shake his hand. This story is officially included in my book at their request because they recognize that their son became better through the intercession of St. Pio.

St. Pio's intercession is very powerful. I consider him one of my patron saints for healing. So, today, instead of praying over a person if somebody asks, I just turn to St. Pio and the Blessed Mother. If ever I am given the feeling that I need to touch them, I will do so, but secretly.

☧

There was this Italian lady from New York whom I met at St. John Neumann Church. She had a good job in management until she was caught shoplifting chocolates from a grocery store. She was fired from her job as a result, and nobody wanted to hire her after that because of her record. She was out of a job for almost three years, was kicked out of her apartment, and there were days when she had no food to eat. Sometimes I gave her $20; other times I brought food to her apartment.

In her desperation, she begged me to pray for her. I told her I would but that even if I prayed for her, nothing would come of it until she changed her ways. She was a very negative person and loved to gossip. I asked St. Pio to intercede for this lady. I prayed that in spite of her police record someone would give her a chance. Then, one night after a particularly long time of prayer in front of St. Pio's statue, I dreamt that she got a job. I told Larry about my dream but he said this time my dream was an impossibility because of her record.

However, my dream was correct. She did get a job offer at J. C. Penney, but told me she didn't like the salary and was going to look for another job. I told her to accept the job and build her reputation as someone trustworthy. Luckily she listened to me. She worked at J. C. Penney for a few months until she was hired by a government agency. She became so reliable at her second job that her boss put her in charge of the office in his absence. She is still working at the same agency and was able to buy a house. I am including her story in this book because she asked me to. She wants my readers to know that through my prayers and my assistance, her life became better. Truly, I prayed hard for her. But everybody needs to recognize that once a person changes her life, God will take over and give that person spiritual as well as material grace. ✞

37
A Heavy Thorn Removed

Larry told me after I immigrated to America in 1996 that he thought it best not to tell his father about Jerilyn and Jerry. He said he didn't know how his father would react. Since my father-in-law was suffering from early-stage cancer, he didn't like to give him any news that could upset him. I wholeheartedly consented. My father-in-law liked me. His wife, Larry's mother, was an immigrant from France. In the eight years I knew him until his death in 2004, I didn't feel anything but kindness from him.

Maryann was 7 when my father-in-law died. She was possibly too young to be affected had I suddenly come out with the truth about myself. But after eight years of secrecy, it was difficult to tell Larry's other relatives and our friends that I had lied to them. Thus I continued lying. No one in the U.S. aside from Larry and my spiritual directors knew about the existence of Jerilyn and Jerry.

Until I had my vision of the Blessed Mother telling me to write a book about my faith story, I was content to deny my Filipino children's existence. I was not too bothered about living a life of hypocrisy. I confessed this dilemma to a priest once and asked him if I was sinning. He responded that so long as my husband knew, it wasn't a sin if I didn't tell others.

In my vision, the Blessed Mother told me: Write your story so that whoever reads it will be inspired by how God allowed your desperate situation in Manila to happen only to intervene and make your life right again when you showed repentance and faith.

To write my faith story meant I had to expose my life in Manila with all its consequences. Before doing so, I had to tell Maryann. But I did not have the courage to tell her. She was already 10 when I had the vision. I slowly added to the 10 pages I initially wrote for her. Three years later, in 2010, I was still writing the book, this time with Father Jim's guidance. Father Jim's advice was for me to start my story from the time I went abroad. He said Maryann was 13 and his concern was how Maryann would react if I told my whole story.

Then Father Jim was assigned to Myanmar before he could finish editing my book. After he left, I continued tinkering with my story, not knowing what to do. I asked the opinion of my next spiritual director, Father Pat. He had the same advice, not to tell Maryann. So I deleted all references to Rolly and the children and tabled the book.

Finally, in August 2012, I turned to my friend Marichelle to help me finish my story. She found the big hole in my account: What happened between 1984 and 1989? What led me to leave the Philippines and go abroad? I told her something bad happened to me in Manila that my two spiritual directors advised me not to mention in order to spare Maryann. Marichelle thought my story lacked depth and conflict. If my purpose in writing the story was to show how God works when a sinner repents, I had to mention not only my venial sins of gossiping but also the bigger sins. However, she said it was my story and she was going to do her best to make it a good read.

The day she and I read her first edited draft, she asked me the meaning of a line she found in my account about the Filipino-American couple in Egypt I had helped. The line mentioned me being in tears when I saw the couple's two toddlers because I remembered the kids I left behind in Manila. As usual I lied when I told her they were my adopted kids. I knew Marichelle could see through me, but again she said it was my story and I had to decide what to include and what to exclude. I went home thinking about why I had missed deleting that line. Was it the Blessed Mother reminding me that if I didn't tell my whole story, I was only half obeying her?

But I was bound to obey my two spiritual directors. That same evening I went back to some of Father Pinto's e-mails to members of DJM. He advised us to choose a spiritual director who has a special devotion to the Blessed Mother, and to follow that director's advice. But Father Pinto also wrote, "with the exception that the directee can follow what she or he thinks is right if God interacts with [her or him], provided that [she or he] prays hard and God will guide [her or him]." I read and re-read Father Pinto's words and prayed hard to Jesus and the Blessed Mother. Deep inside me I heard the words: Come clean and confess in the book.

On November 28, I attended Mass and a novena to Our Mother of Perpetual Help before heading to work. I planned to tell Maryann about Jerilyn and Jerry sometime soon, so I prayed to the Blessed Mother to put the right words in my mouth when I did so. After work that day, I was supposed to go back to OMPH Church for a prayer group meeting, but my feet became very painful and I could hardly walk. I was in heels all day at work but I knew that was not the reason my feet hurt. I was being reminded by the Blessed Mother to go home and talk to Maryann instead of going to the prayer group.

First I asked Maryann if she was aware I was writing my life's story in obedience to a vision I'd had of the Blessed Mother. She said yes. I told her it was almost finished but I had one concern. She needed to know that Jerilyn and Jerry in the Philippines were not really adopted as we'd made her believe.

"They are my real kids from another man," I said. I told her this man had forced me and even though I did not like him, I had to stay with him; that we were never legally married; and that because he was bad I had to run as far away as I could from him.

"I met your dad and I didn't really like to be married at that time but my spiritual director who is a very holy priest told me that I needed to marry your dad because he is a very good man."

183

While I was blurting all this out to her, Maryann calmly waited for me to tell her everything. I told her God was giving me another chance and her father understood that it was not my choice to be in relation with this man who took advantage of me.

"Now you know the reason why I'm very strict with you if you are talking with teenage boys, especially if we don't know them. They could harm you and I don't want you to go through what happened to me." I told her I was not prayerful while in Manila. I emphasized the importance of prayers and of wearing holy medals for protection from any harm.

I ended with, "Maryann, if I'm very strict with you, it's because I care for you very much and you might not understand that. If there is a situation that I have to choose between your life and mine, I will choose to die so that you will survive. That is how a mother loves her kids."

Finally my 15-year-old Maryann smiled. "It's OK, Mommy. I just don't want you to lie anymore. Even if my friends will know about it, it will not affect me."

Telling her the truth was like a big painful thorn had been pulled from my heart. We were trying to protect Maryann from knowing the truth, but it turned out that Maryann did not need to be protected. She is mature beyond her years.

After I went to Marichelle with my whole story, she made changes in the first draft. We also added Chapter 6, "Lost in Manila," and this chapter to complete it. ✟

38
The Rest of My Life

I intend to keep to my plan and purpose of life that I submitted to the DJM in 2011. I will continue the religious practices like fasting and abstaining. On first Fridays, I try not to work because I have allotted that day for fasting and prayer. I start the day with Mass followed by the adoration of the Blessed Sacrament. I drink water and, if ever I eat, I take only one piece of bread all day. I break my fast at midnight. During Lent I abstain from meat, until Easter.

Larry and I will continue to be members of the Legion of Mary and the Cenacle prayer group. We will continue our Wednesday novenas to Our Mother of Perpetual Help. I will still serve as an extraordinary Eucharistic minister. I will not stop praying for the conversion of sinners.

I will continue working as a substitute teacher and occasional teacher's aide in Lancaster County. Besides teaching regular students, I will continue teaching children with multiple disabilities as one way to serve God.

I will continue to help my Filipino children as well as other relatives because I recognize that my money is God's money, and that besides supporting my family, God wants me to extend my help to others.

Larry and I will continue to support religious orders that spread the good news about God.

I will also continue to evangelize people who have little knowledge of God's mercy. This is why I've written this book. I was a great sinner, God forgave me, and I found peace through the sacrament of confession and reconciliation. I recommend a practice of going to confession once a month, either on First Saturday in honor of the Blessed

Mother or on First Friday in honor of the Sacred Heart of Jesus. The more we go to confession, even just for venial sins, the more the Holy Spirit will give us strength to overcome temptations.

Besides the Santo Niño, the Blessed Mother, Pope John Paul II, and St. John Neumann, there are other saints I turn to for intercession. I pray to St. Martha when I'm cooking and doing household chores; to St. Anthony for direction when I am lost or to help me find lost objects; to St. Benedict for physical protection; to St. Joseph for my husband's peace of mind; to St. Pio for healing; to St. Teresa of Jesus; to St. Therese, the Little Flower; and last but not least to St. Josephine Bakhita.

Sometimes I also ask the Holy Souls in purgatory to intercede on my behalf. One of them is Father Abel, who died in a terrible accident. Very often when I ask for his intercession, my prayers are granted. Father Abel always told me to ask for prayers from people who are holy because God listens to them. This is because holy people always follow God's commandments and are living saints.

We all have the same purpose in life—to try to live in the state of grace and strive to be saints. ✞

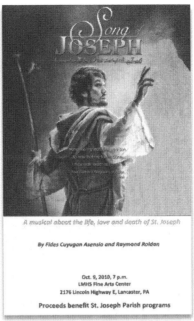

Song of Joseph playbill

Song of Joseph cast welcome at Lint home, October 4, 2010, for October 9 U.S. premiere performance

Linda's personal pilgrim Fatima statue, purchased in old Jerusalem, then used in Egypt and Maryland

Linda serving as extraordinary minister of Holy Communion, Sacristy of Our Mother of Perpetual Help Church, Ephrata, March 11, 2007

Linda at Scrabble tournament in Lancaster, July 2002

Rosary procession at the National Centre for Padre Pio,
Barto, Pennsylvania, October 3, 2009

✝

"Pray, hope, and don't worry."

St. Pio of Pietrelcina

About the Co-Authors

Marichelle Roque-Lutz started her journalism career in her native Philippines. She was chief editor of the weekly magazine *Woman's Home Companion.* She also co-authored the book *Free Within Prison Walls,* the story of Roger Arienda, a Filipino political firebrand who found Jesus Christ while in prison. In the United States, she was a copy editor as well as religion editor of the *Intelligencer Journal,* the morning daily of Lancaster County, Pennsylvania. She retired in 2006.

The Rev. James W. Kofski, a Minnesota native, lived in the Philippines for five years. He taught English in the Cagayan Valley and completed an M.A. at the University of the Philippines with a focus on Southeast Asian Studies. After writing about agriculture for 10 years in the United States, he entered Maryknoll. He was ordained in 1991 in New York and has been assigned to Cairo, Jerusalem, Bangkok, and Washington, D.C. He currently lives in Myanmar. ✞

Acknowledgments

I would like to thank the Rev. James W. Kofski, the Rev. Patrick McGarrity, and Monsignor Thomas Smith for their spiritual direction in my life. Additional thanks go to Father Kofski for his encouragement and early-stage arrangement of my story.

Many thanks to Marichelle Roque-Lutz for her hard work in focusing my story. Through her efforts this book was finally made ready for publication.

I thank my husband, Larry, for his unflagging faith in my visions and his wholehearted belief that I have been called to write this book. Thank you, Larry, for helping me remember events, names, and places and for your many hours spent reading and rereading the manuscript.

Last but not least, I thank my 15-year-old daughter, Maryann, for her maturity to understand and accept events that happened in my earlier life. She is the final inspiration that pushed me to finish the last chapters of this book. ♱

Made in the USA
Columbia, SC
14 April 2018